MAKE YOUR OWN

KNIFE HANDLES

STEP-BY-STEP TECHNIQUES *for* CUSTOMIZING YOUR BLADE

MAKE YOUR OWN
KNIFE HANDLES

STEP-BY-STEP TECHNIQUES *for* CUSTOMIZING YOUR BLADE

CHRIS GLEASON

SPRING HOUSE PRESS

Publisher: Paul McGahren
Editorial Director: Matthew Teague
Copy Editor: Kerri Grzybicki
Design: Lindsay Hess
Layout: Chad McClung
Step-by-Step Photography: Chris Gleason
Project Photography: Danielle Atkins

Spring House Press
P.O. Box 239
Whites Creek, TN 37189

ISBN: 978-1-940611-53-2
Library of Congress Control Number: 2017950963
Printed in the United States of America
First Printing: October 2017

Note:
The following list contains names used in *Make Your Own Knife Handles* that may be registered with the United States Copyright Office: Barlow; Bon Ami; Fiji; Hock; Sarge; Swiss Army; Wood River; Work Sharp; Zhen.

To learn more about Spring House Press books, or to find a retailer near you, email *info@springhousepress.com* or visit us at *www.springhousepress.com*.

CONTENTS

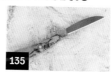

INTRODUCTION

I remember seeing my first knife kit a couple of years ago in our local woodworking store, and it seemed like a terrific idea. Knife kits are perfect for woodworkers at all levels of experience; beginners will find them to be a great introductory project with some unique technical challenges, and veterans will enjoy crafting one-of-a-kind knives that they'll cherish forever. Knife kits also make great gifts—who wouldn't like to receive a knife with a gorgeous custom handle?

Writing this book was a joy, as I got to sample the range of kits that have recently been introduced. Are you mesmerized by the organic look of Damascus steel, like I am? They've got you covered. Are you a hunter who might prize making your own knife to take into the field? Check. Maybe you'd like a hatchet to take camping—yup, that's in here, too. So I'd like to think that this book has a bit of "something for everyone." I also tried to present a range of techniques for making and attaching handles, as I realize that people have different tools available to them, and I wanted to be as inclusive as possible. Who knows? You may even come up with some techniques that I haven't thought of.

One of the best parts of the process, of course, is choosing the material for your handles. Whether you want something simple or something eye-catching, it's your call. When I saw the kits for the first time, I imagined that people could even use wood from their own backyards, or some other interesting or meaningful source. Lo and behold, I was not too surprised when I recently taught a course on making knife handles, and a few students brought in some figured maple that one of them had "rescued" from a chunk of firewood. Now those were some custom knives with a unique history behind them! I'm sure those guys will be telling that story for years to come.

Have fun and stay sharp,
Chris Gleason

CHAPTER 1
KITCHEN KNIVES

A kitchen knife is a great project to start with if you haven't made your own knife handle yet. A chef's knife or paring knife are both good basic projects that can also provide a great showcase for your skills as you improve. If you'd like to try something more unusual, turn to the ulu knife project on page 53. No matter what project you choose, you'll be adding a unique and useful tool to your kitchen rotation!

8" CHEF'S KNIFE

A knife that belongs in every kitchen

MATERIALS & TOOLS

- › Chef knife kit, ⅛" thick x 8"
- › Wood of choice
- › Tablesaw
- › Planer
- › Clamps
- › Pencil
- › Jigsaw or bandsaw
- › Epoxy
- › Drill press
- › Drill bit, ¼"
- › Belt sander or sanding block
- › Chisel
- › Random-orbit belt sander
- › Vise (optional)
- › Wood finish of choice

I'm a huge fan of custom chef's knives. They're my favorite knives to make, and with good reason: I cook most of our meals, so I get a daily dose of satisfaction when it's time to slice and dice. There are a number of chef's knife kits on the market, but for this one I chose a blade with O1 steel—a top-notch choice when it comes to holding a sharp edge for a long time. And the traditional shape of this blade ensures that this knife will never go out of style. Use any material you like for the handle, although I happen to think that a darker wood—I used wenge—creates an appealing contrast against the matte steel.

— 1 —

Plan it out. Take measurements for the handle blank noting the length, width, and overall thickness (including the blade). It's a good idea to add ¼" to the length and width so that you have a little wiggle room later. You'll want to be as close as possible on the thickness—if it helps, measure some of the knives that you have around the house to decide what feels best in your hand.

— 2 —

Smooth one edge. Choose a length of 1"-thick stock to create the handle for your knife. Then use your jointer or a hand plane to smooth and straighten one edge of the board.

— 3 —

Cut it to width. On the tablesaw, rip a long length of stock to the desired width. The extra length allows you to keep your fingers safe during the next step.

— 4 —

Smooth out the blank. Back at the jointer, flatten one face of the handle blank. This is where the extra length helps out, so your fingers never get too close to the blade. Push sticks are a must.

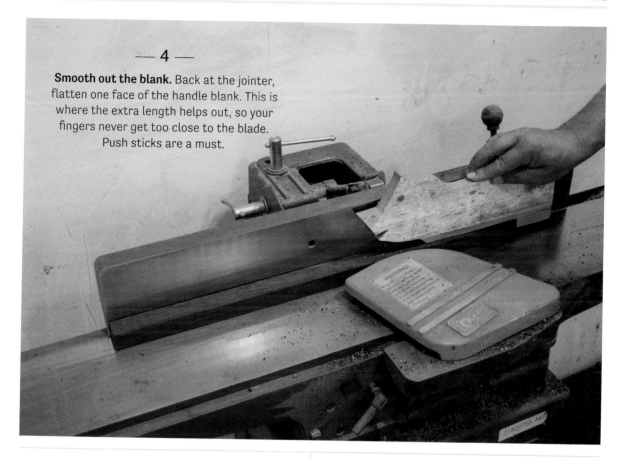

— 5 —

Split the blank in two. With the blank turned on its edge, measure to find the center and rip the stock into two equal halves. You can almost imagine the tablesaw blade creating a kerf where the knife blade will be sandwiched. Don't worry about the saw marks at this point—they'll be sanded out later.

— 6 —

Cut out the blanks. With two pieces of handle stock stacked on top of each other, and the length marked out, use a miter saw or handsaw to cut them to length.

— 7 —

Double-check your blanks. Once the blanks are cut down to size, you can start to visualize how the handle comes together.

— 8 —

Mark it out. Use a permanent marker to trace the profile of the knife's handle onto one of the blank's inside faces. It's a good idea to add ⅛" of extra room—it is easier to sand away the excess than to start over from scratch because the wood was cut too aggressively.

— 9 —

Saw it to shape. Use either a bandsaw or jigsaw to cut the blank to rough shape. If using a jigsaw, clamp the workpiece in place and cut half of the shape. With a jigsaw, err on cutting outside the line to compensate for any possible bend in the blade.

—10—

Change position. Once one end of the blank is cut to shape, flip it around, clamp it in place, and finish making the cut.

—11—

Mark one side from the other. Once one side of the handle is cut to shape, position it over the mating blank, and draw out the pattern. Then cut it to rough shape.

—12—

Take note of grain patterns. To create a handle with matching grain across the blanks, make sure to note which sides face inward. Sometimes it's the little things . . .

—13—

Lay on the glue. Attach the first side of the handle blank with epoxy. If you haven't worked with two-part epoxy, you simply mix the two parts together to activate it. Once mixed, slather a generous layer onto the wood.

—14—

Clamp it up. Clamp the handle blank to the blade on a flat surface—a scrap of wood or even your benchtop with waxed paper underneath to catch glue squeeze-out works well. Though many epoxies claim a 5-minute cure time, wait a bit longer before removing the clamps—about 30 minutes is good.

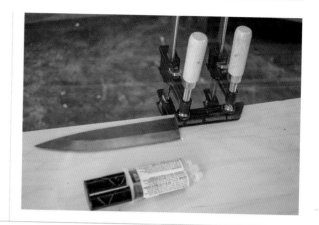

—15—

Drill it out. When drilling holes for the pins, position the bit to go through the piloted holes in the blade and into the handle blank. To get the pins to fit properly later, your drill press must be set for exactly 90°. Position a flat wooden block on the underside of the workpiece to prevent tear-out.

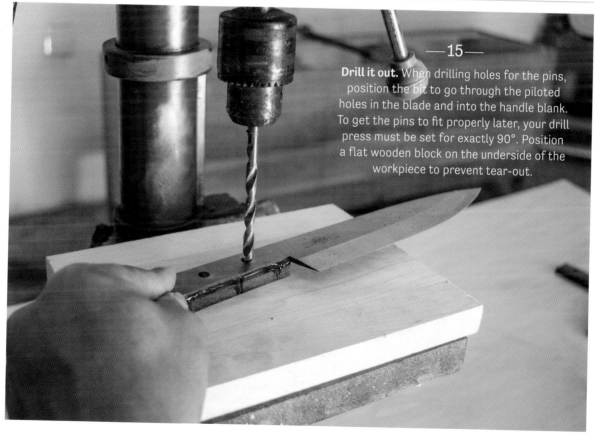

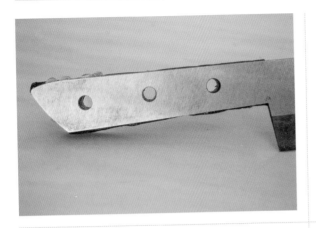

—16—

Check your work. Because you used the holes in the blank to position the drill bit, the holes in the blank should align perfectly with those in the blade blank.

—17—

Glue on the second side. Begin gluing on the second side of the handle by mixing up a batch of epoxy and spreading a coat on the blade.

—18—

Clamp up the handle. Use a clamp—or as shown here, an old machinist's vise—to hold the parts together as the epoxy cures.

—19—

Drill all the way through. After the epoxy dries, go back to the drill press and drill through the first set of holes and into the newly applied blank. If your setup is dialed in at 90°, everything should line up automatically.

—20—

Prepare for pins. To install the pins, apply a healthy coat of epoxy into the holes. The blade kit used here comes with a pair of ¼"-diameter stainless steel pins that are a great complement to the blade, but you could substitute different pin material if you like.

—21—

Set the pins in place. The pins should fit snugly in the holes, going in with only a few taps but without excess slop in around their edges.

—22—

Drive home the pins. A little bit of hammering sets the pins flush with the wood. Be gentle and precise with the hammer to avoid marring the wooden handle.

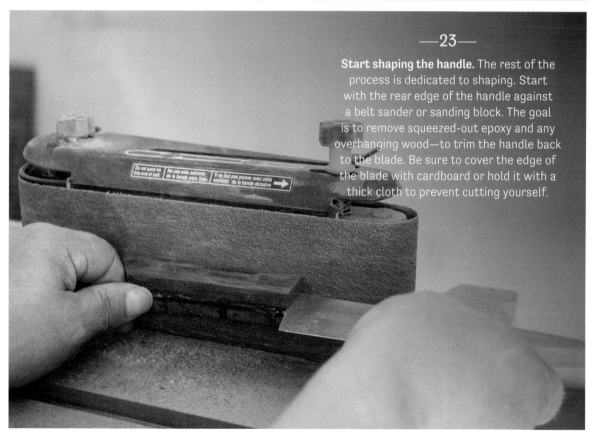

—23—

Start shaping the handle. The rest of the process is dedicated to shaping. Start with the rear edge of the handle against a belt sander or sanding block. The goal is to remove squeezed-out epoxy and any overhanging wood—to trim the handle back to the blade. Be sure to cover the edge of the blade with cardboard or hold it with a thick cloth to prevent cutting yourself.

—24—

Shape the heel. The profile at the bottom of the handle (the heel) has a slight curve that can be shaped with either a belt sander or a large, flat sanding block.

—25—

Get creative. It helps to use the small radius on the end of the belt sander to get into some of the hard-to-reach nooks and crannies on the handle.

—26—

Smooth the sides. Once you've gotten as close as possible around the front edge, the back edge, and the bottom of the handle, you can focus on the sides of the handle. It is pretty satisfying to see the pins finally poke through.

—27—

Tackle the trouble spots. Getting into the nook below the blade needs to be done by hand. Machines can help, but they can't do it all.

—28—

Keep it symmetrical. The goal with the back of the handle is to remove nice, even amounts of stock so that the edges and sides of the handle are still at 90° to each other.

—29—

Pull out the hand tools. You can use a random orbit sander to at least get close, but the final cut is easiest with a good, sharp chisel. It quickly pares away the adhesive and the remaining wood.

—30—

Aim for consistency. The goal of sanding and shaping is to get a clean, even reveal so that the blade thickness appears uniform throughout and so that you don't cut into or distort its profile.

—31—

Soften it up. To ease the sharp edges of the handle, you can use either a belt sander or a small sanding block. If you're using a belt sander, lift the handle off the worktable and rotate it carefully to create a roundover between the sides and the edges.

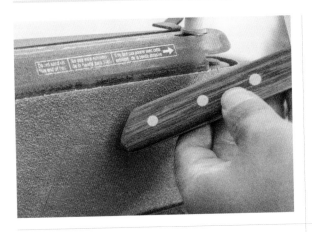

—32—

Continue the roundover. The heel is approached in the same way as the sides. Aim for a consistent radius as you soften all the edges.

—33—

Create a transition. For a handle that feels more comfortable in your hand, taper the handle down to where the blade begins. The small end of the belt sander works great for this.

—34—

Shape both sides the same way. The tapers should appear symmetrical when viewed from either top or bottom.

—35—

Soften things up. Use a chisel to ease the edges of the tapers and blend them into the handle more seamlessly.

—36—

Finish it off. The handle can be finished with your favorite finish. The knife shown here was finished with three coats of oil-based polyurethane and sanded between each coats. As with all wood-handled knives, keep this gem out of the dishwasher.

SANDING SMART

Making a knife handle is a relatively small project, but the process requires a lot of sanding—by both hand and power—which generates a great deal of dust. Always remember to protect your lungs, eyes, and ears. You can protect your lungs by wearing a dust mask or, better yet, a respirator. You should also collect dust at the source when possible. Toward that end (and not shown in the photo) there is a shop vacuum hooked up to the dust port on the back of the sander. Safety glasses helps prevent dust from getting into your eyes, and earplugs or earmuffs will protect your ears against the drone of power sanders.

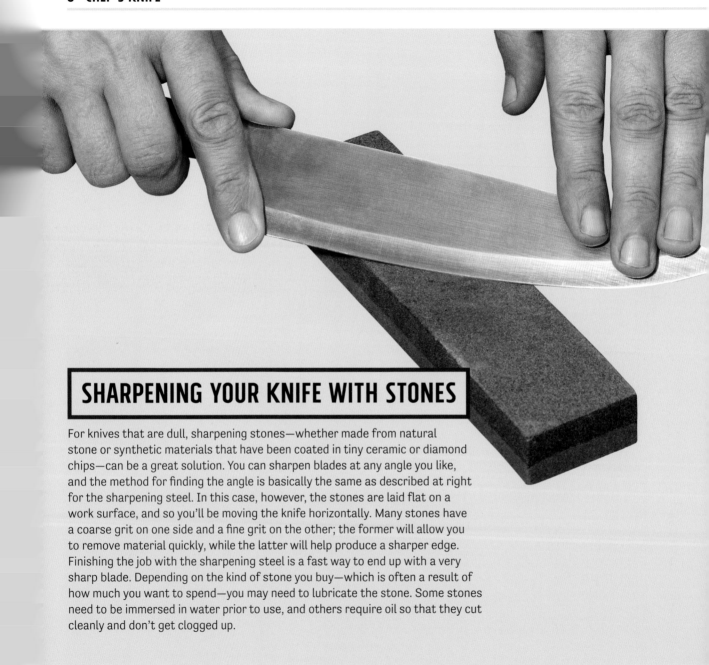

SHARPENING YOUR KNIFE WITH STONES

For knives that are dull, sharpening stones—whether made from natural stone or synthetic materials that have been coated in tiny ceramic or diamond chips—can be a great solution. You can sharpen blades at any angle you like, and the method for finding the angle is basically the same as described at right for the sharpening steel. In this case, however, the stones are laid flat on a work surface, and so you'll be moving the knife horizontally. Many stones have a coarse grit on one side and a fine grit on the other; the former will allow you to remove material quickly, while the latter will help produce a sharper edge. Finishing the job with the sharpening steel is a fast way to end up with a very sharp blade. Depending on the kind of stone you buy—which is often a result of how much you want to spend—you may need to lubricate the stone. Some stones need to be immersed in water prior to use, and others require oil so that they cut cleanly and don't get clogged up.

USING A SHARPENING STEEL

For day-in and day-out maintenance of an already sharpened blade, a sharpening steel is hard to beat. Often sold with knife sets, but also available as stand-alone items, sharpening steels don't have the ability to put an edge on a really dull knife, but they are ideal for honing a knife that has started to lose its edge. How do they work? Sharpening steels are finely textured—sometimes with the addition of ceramic or diamond abrasives—so they can realign the steel along a blade's edge. How often should you do it? As soon as you feel your knife not cutting as well as it used to. This might mean once per week, once per month, or a couple of times per day, depending on your use.

To use a sharpening steel, begin by holding it vertically with the tip down on a cutting board. Then hold your knife out against the steel, tilting it at the necessary angle. Most knives are sharpened at 20°. How do you figure this out? Start by holding the knife at 90° to the steel. Then divide this in half, by eye. You'll be at 45°. Divide this in half and you'll be holding it at 22.5°. A small rotation of the wrist toward the steel should get you at right about 20°. You'll then make a few gentle strokes across the steel, alternating from one side to the other. It doesn't take much force at all, and only about six strokes per side.

DAMASCUS STEEL CHEF'S KNIFE

Alluring blade and simple handle

MATERIALS & TOOLS

> Chef knife kit
> Pre-made scales of wood of choice about ⅜" x 1½" x 5"
> Tablesaw
> Planer
> Clamps
> Pencil
> Bandsaw
> Epoxy
> Drill press and ⅛" bit
> Router with guide bushing
> Belt sander
> Random-orbit belt sander with 80- through 400-grit pads
> Vise
> Wood finish of choice

This is an incredible knife. I've been making knives, from scratch, for 5 years now, and even I am fully in awe of this one. You pretty much can't do better. So if you're a serious cook, or want to make a gift for someone who is, look no further than a Damascus blade. It comes sharp right out of the box, and the unmistakable look of Damascus steel is always alluring.

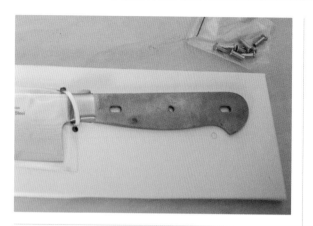

Inspect the blade. This particular knife kit features a nicely sculpted bolster that your handle material will butt up against. You'll then shape the wood to match it, which creates an elegant look.

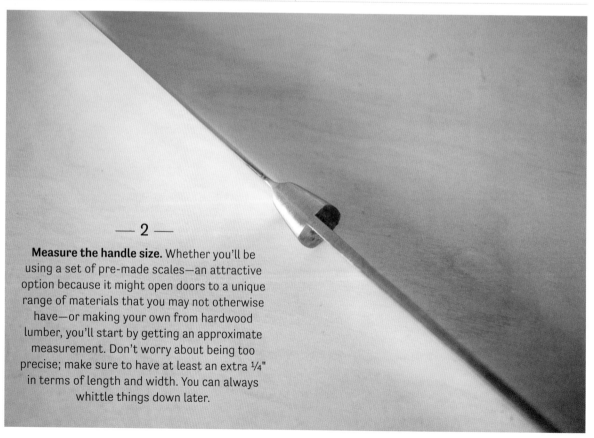

— 2 —

Measure the handle size. Whether you'll be using a set of pre-made scales—an attractive option because it might open doors to a unique range of materials that you may not otherwise have—or making your own from hardwood lumber, you'll start by getting an approximate measurement. Don't worry about being too precise; make sure to have at least an extra ¼" in terms of length and width. You can always whittle things down later.

— 3 —

Cut your blank to width. When choosing your handle, select a material that will make a good color contrast with the steel. Walnut is pictured here. Beware any flashy grain pattern that distracts from the Damascus steel itself.

— 4 —

Rip the blank in half. After cutting the blank to width, turn it on edge (90°) and rip two pieces to approximately 5/16"-thick.

— 5 —

Check the thickness. The wood should be proud of the steel by no more than 3/32". Keep it as precise as you can so that you save yourself the hassle of having to remove a lot of stock later.

— 6 —

Reduce the thickness. Using a thickness planer makes short work of sizing the stock for the handle.

— 7 —

Check the thickness.
Clamp the handle blank to the knife and ensure that it fllush with the bolster on the blade. This is a perfect fit.

— 8 —

Trace the handle. With the thickness established, start imagining the profile you'll be cutting out. Trace the handle onto the wood and cut it out with your bandsaw. Epoxy one half of the wood to the knife.

Drill a test hole. Drill a test hole in scrap wood before doing so on the actual knife handle. Select the drill bit size closest to the pins. For this kit, a ⅛" bit is required.

—10—

Check the pin fit.
When the blank is drilled to the correct diameter, the pin will slide into the hole smoothly using only a bit of hand pressure.

— 11 —

Drill the pin holes. Assured that your pins will fit neatly, use the drill press to drill holes through the first layer of walnut. Drill directly through the blade handle and into the wooden blank, which guarantees that the holes will be perfectly aligned.

— 12 —

Remove the waste. Because this knife is fairly long, you can clamp it to the edge of a workbench and remove the waste from the blank with a router equipped with a guide bushing. Just be sure to protect the blade with cardboard or a thick layer of paper towels. For more detail on the routing process, refer to the hatchet project on page 127.

Check the handle. Routing the handle flush is quick work that generates very precise results. No router? Simply sand the handle flush to the blade.

—14—

Epoxy the second half. Gluing down the second half of the handle is a simple matter—just mix up a batch of 5-minute epoxy, lay on a thin coat, and clamp the handle in place.

—15—

Remove the waste. After the epoxy cures, use your router to remove the excess wood as before. Again, if you don't have a router or the correct bit and bushing, sanding works as well.

—16—

Extend the pin holes. Back at the drill press, extend the holes all the way through the knife.

—17—

Begin sanding. The router did a very clean job on the outline, so a couple minutes on the belt sander cleaned things up nicely.

—18—

Complete sanding. Use a random-orbit sander to fine-tune the handle and ease the edges. It also works nicely on the transition between the bolster and the wooden scales. Start with 80 grit and work up through 400.

—19—

Add pins and finish. Epoxy the pins and use your vise to squeeze them in. You can see what a handsome project this knife is. Finish the handle as desired.

WHAT EXACTLY IS DAMASCUS STEEL?

If you've looked around at fine kitchen knives in the last few years, you've probably come across the distinctive look of "Damascus Steel." But what exactly is it, and what's the history behind it? Well, it turns out to be a very old technique for forging sharp and durable blades. It takes its name from the city of Damascus in the city of Syria, which is one of the oldest cities in the world. As the city was located near key trade routes between Europe and the Far East, bladesmiths in Damascus came into possession of something called Wootz steel, which was imported from India, and was developed around 300 BC. These raw blanks (or billets) of steel came to be known as Damascus steel in later years. The billets are formed by forge-welding layers of steel together. During the forge-welding process, a smith heats two or more layers of steel and joins them by hammering them together. After further heating, the billet can be folded back onto itself and hammered down to create very intricate patterns. An experienced smith can use different types of steel and iron to produce a billet with the specific qualities that they desire. The best blades have always enjoyed the reputation of holding a sharp edge for a very long time, and of course they're quite lovely as well.

8" SLICING/CARVING KNIFE

Perfect for slicing any meat

MATERIALS & TOOLS

> Slicing/carving knife kit
> Wood of choice
> Tablesaw
> Jointer
> Planer
> Spring clamps (2)
> Pencil or marker
> Bandsaw
> Epoxy
> Drill press
> Drill bit, ¼"
> Belt sander
> Random-orbit sander
> Wood finish of choice

This is the knife you pull out around the holidays to impress the guests. Need to slice up that turkey? No problem. If you're more into Tofurkey—well, I'm sure this knife is up to that challenge as well. For this project I used a kit with a blade made from top quality, high carbon O1 tool steel, which allows it to be finely sharpened and hold an edge for a long time.

— 1 —

Angle the end. Start with a length of stock (ironwood is used here) large enough to create two sides of the knife handle. Then, at the miter saw, cut one end to fit the angle of the steel if needed.

— 2 —

Cut out the blanks. After tracing the handle's profile onto the 5/16"-thick stock, use a bandsaw equipped with a 1/4", 6 tpi blade to free the handle from the blank. Err on the side of making the blank too large—you can always sand away the excess, but you can't add any extra.

— 3 —

Lay on the epoxy. Mix and spread a thin layer of 5-minute epoxy onto the wood blank and then set it in place on the handle portion of the blade.

— 4 —

Clamp it up. Two spring clamps provide more than enough force to hold the parts together and prevent slipping before the glue sets.

— 5 —

Prepare the second side. Once the glue cures, trace the knife handle onto the stock you're using for the other side of the handle. Before moving on, be sure to drill through the metal and all the way through the wood on the handle. This prevents you from covering up—and losing, for good—the holes needed for the pins.

— 6 —

Glue up the second side. Lay on another coat of 5-minute epoxy and set the remaining side of the handle in place. Use a few spring clamps to hold the wood-metal-wood sandwich together until the glue dries.

— 7 —

Clean it up. A belt sander excels at flattening large areas quickly. After allowing the epoxy enough time to set up, use a belt sander to remove the excess wood.

— 8 —

The belt sander can also be used to chamfer long edges. This chamfer is a preliminary step to rounding over the edges, but if you prefer the angular look, you could stop at this stage.

— 9 —

Round it off. A random-orbit sander does a good job of knocking off the hard edges on the handle, but you could create the same effect with a sanding block. When shaping the handle, stop frequently to check for symmetry and test out how the shape feels in your hand.

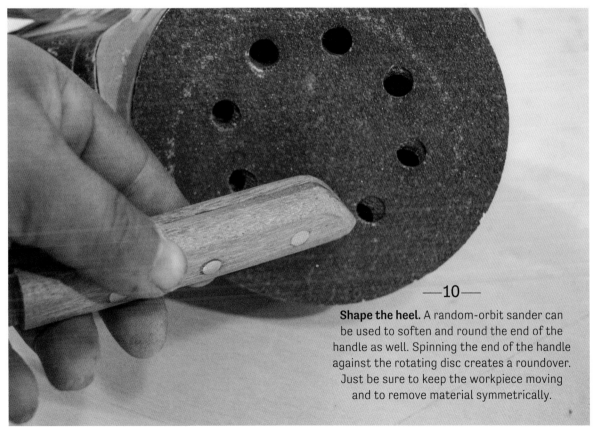

—10—

Shape the heel. A random-orbit sander can be used to soften and round the end of the handle as well. Spinning the end of the handle against the rotating disc creates a roundover. Just be sure to keep the workpiece moving and to remove material symmetrically.

PARING KNIFE

A small knife delivers big work

MATERIALS & TOOLS

- › Paring knife kit
- › Wood of choice
- › Tablesaw
- › Jointer
- › Planer
- › Spring clamps (2)
- › Pencil
- › Jigsaw or bandsaw
- › Epoxy
- › Stationary belt sander or sanding block
- › Wood finish of choice

My wife and I are a modern couple—with all of the flexibility that sometimes entails—and so one of my chores is to prepare our dinners. Fine with me, since this guarantees that I always get to eat whatever I'm in the mood for. Chef's choice, right? Anyway, part of keeping me happy and productive in the kitchen is having the right tool for the job—and while our new waffle iron is admittedly just a fun bonus, basics like knives are essential. This paring knife is truly one to lust after. It is made from the same Damascus steel as the chef's knife on page 29, so whether you're considering it for yourself or somebody else, it is always nice to have a complete set. Both knives will last a lifetime and then some.

— 1 —

Quality materials are key. Start by choosing a quality kit that can hold a good edge. The sycamore used for the handle on this knife was culled from a whole sycamore tree that was sawn into lumber.

— 2 —

Prepare the handle stock. Give the stock a few passes across the jointer to clean up and square two adjacent faces. With small pieces of stock, be sure to use push sticks to keep your hands safely away from the blades.

— 3 —

Separate the handle stock. Rip down the center of the handle stock to separate it into two strips that are each 5⁄16" thick. Note: You'll need to use a zero clearance insert for this type of cut.

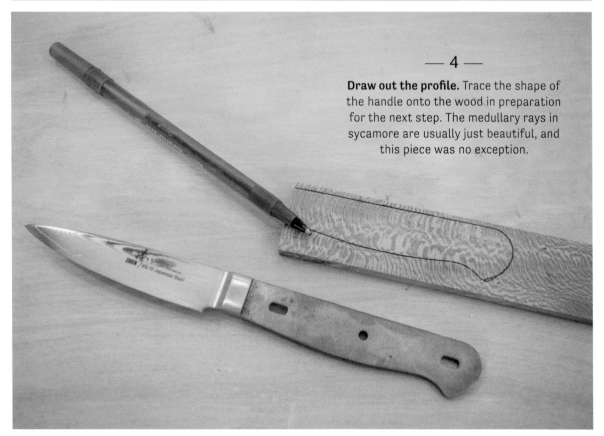

— 4 —

Draw out the profile. Trace the shape of the handle onto the wood in preparation for the next step. The medullary rays in sycamore are usually just beautiful, and this piece was no exception.

— 5 —

Cut it out. A bandsaw, scrollsaw, or jigsaw are all good choices for cutting out the shape of the handle on the handle blank. Even a coping saw would work fine.

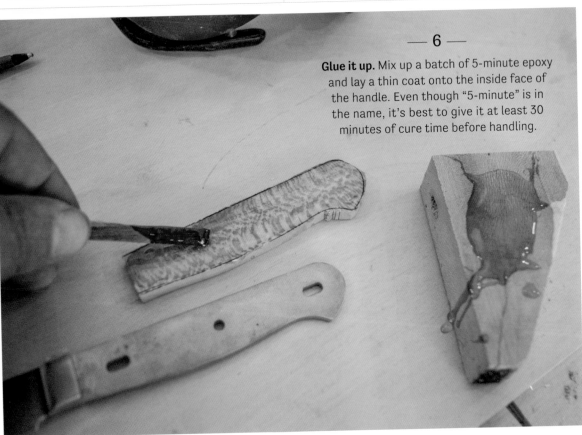

— 6 —

Glue it up. Mix up a batch of 5-minute epoxy and lay a thin coat onto the inside face of the handle. Even though "5-minute" is in the name, it's best to give it at least 30 minutes of cure time before handling.

— 7 —

Clamp it in place. Set the handle in place on the knife and position it so that there's a small wooden edge exposed on all sides of the metal. Use a few spring clamps to secure it in place while the glue sets.

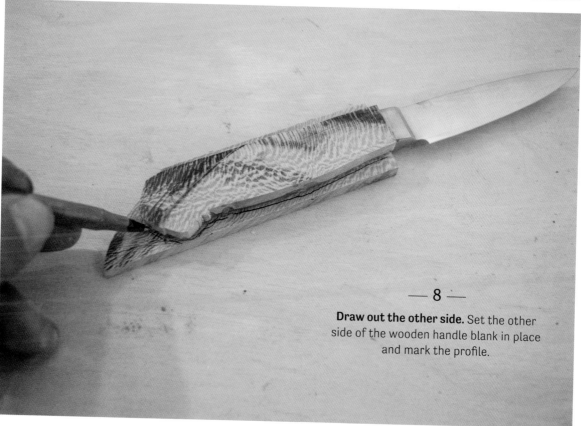

— 8 —

Draw out the other side. Set the other side of the wooden handle blank in place and mark the profile.

— 9 —

Saw it out. As before, use your saw of choice—in this case, a jigsaw is shown—to cut out the second side of the blank. Cut as close as you can to the line without going inside the line.

—10—

Bring it all together. Mix another small batch of epoxy and attach the other side of the handle to the blade. Spring clamps are easy to maneuver and offer plenty of strength to hold everything together.

—11—

Use a stationary belt sander or hand-held **sanding block to sand the wood flush to the metal.** Then soften the edges to whatever degree feels good in your hand. For more detail on handle shaping, see page 99.

PUT YOUR NEW KNIFE TO WORK

Gleason's Famous Apple Strudel

There's no way I can legitimately call this strudel "famous"—it seldom makes it past our own backyard—and it is barely even "Gleason's" since I more or less based it on all the other flaky, apple-filled German pastries I've eaten in the past. But at least I admit it; as they say in the world of baking, we're all standing on the strudels of giants.

Ingredients:

4 apples, peeled, cored, and sliced

1 cup of brown sugar

1 cup of raisins (optional, but highly recommended)

1 sheet frozen puff pastry, thawed

1 egg

¼ cup milk

Instructions:

Preheat oven to 400°F (200°C). Line a baking sheet with parchment paper.

Place apples in a large bowl. Stir in brown sugar and golden raisins; set aside. Place puff pastry on baking sheet. Roll lightly with a rolling pin. Arrange apple filling down the middle of the pastry lengthwise. Fold the pastry lengthwise around the mixture. Seal edges of pastry by using a bit of water on your fingers, and rubbing the pastry edges together. Whisk egg and milk together, and brush onto top of pastry.

For artistic measure, make a few slits (3 or 4) on top of the strudel. These will open up and look cool as it bakes.

Bake in preheated oven for 35 to 40 minutes, or until golden brown.

ALASKAN ULU

A unique design with countless uses

MATERIALS & TOOLS

> › Ulu knife kit
> › Wood of choice
> › Jointer
> › Planer
> › Tablesaw
> › Clamp
> › Pencil or marker
> › Bandsaw
> › Epoxy
> › Drill press
> › Drill bit, ⅛"
> › Drill bit, ¼"
> › Hand sanding block
> › Wood finish of choice

I hadn't used an ulu prior to making a handle for this one. But now I totally get it. And I love this thing. If you're not especially familiar, here's a little background. An ulu is a multi-purpose knife traditionally used by Inuit, Yup'ik, and Aleut women. It is utilized in applications as diverse as skinning and cleaning animals, cutting a child's hair, cutting food, and, if necessary, trimming blocks of snow and ice used to build an igloo. I've just used mine in the kitchen, but that's a pretty impressive resume, for sure.

— 1 —

Create a pattern. Start by marking a center line on paper and sketching a profile that looks good to your eye. Before removing the blade, mark the location of the holes. You can see that the hole on the left of the blade is actually an elongated oval. This provides a little wiggle room in case something is off later on.

— 2 —

Make symmetry automatic. Rather than trying to draw a symmetrical pattern freehand, fold the paper in half and trace the initial line on the back of the left-hand side of the paper. This is an old but handy trick.

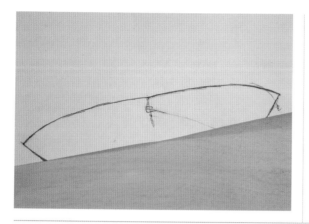

— 3 —

Fold it up. With the paper unfolded, trace the line on the back of the left-hand side of the paper so that you have a continuous line. Easy peasy.

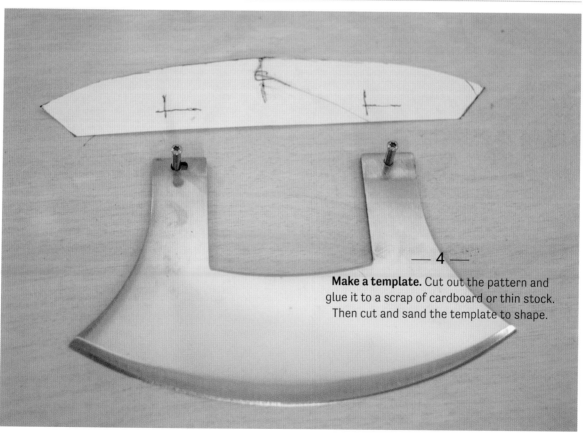

— 4 —

Make a template. Cut out the pattern and glue it to a scrap of cardboard or thin stock. Then cut and sand the template to shape.

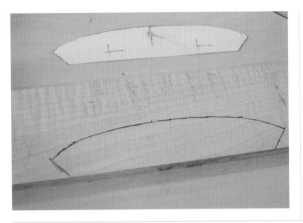

— 5 —

Draw it out. Trace the template outline onto the wood blank you plan to use. The handle shown here is made of curly maple that is milled to $1\frac{1}{16}$" thick.

— 6 —

Cut away the waste. Make a rip cut at the tablesaw to cut away the excess. Then turn the blank on edge and rip the future handle into two sides. With a piece of curly maple like this, avoid making unnecessary cuts so that the unused stock remains as large as possible. Once you cut through the blank, hold the wood securely, turn off the saw, and wait until the blade stops turning.

— 7 —

Drill for the pins. While the pieces are still connected, move to the drill press and bore holes for the barrel bolts. If your two sides of the handle are already cut apart, simply stack them up so that when you drill, the holes are aligned on both sides.

— 8 —

Cut the handle to shape. Use a jigsaw to cut the two sides of the handle to shape. A bandsaw would work as well.

— 9 —

Countersink the holes. The fasteners needed to be lightly countersunk with a ¼" drill bit, which is best done at the drill press.

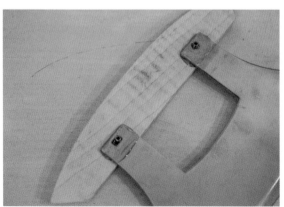

—10—

Set the bolts in place. Before clamping, lay on a little 5-minute epoxy and tighten the bolts immediately to lock everything into place—once the epoxy dries, there'll be no chance of the parts moving.

—11—

A single clamp is plenty. Glue up the whole assembly at one time. The key is not to overdo it with the epoxy so you avoid cleaning up a big mess of glue squeeze-out. Apply just enough glue and use lacquer thinner to clean up any squeeze-out immediately. After the epoxy cures, only a bit of light sanding is required.

WHAT IS AN ULU?

Ulu knives were developed in the Arctic region at least 3,500 years ago. They were then used to clean and fillet fish, skin hides, process meat, and make clothing from skins. Talk about a versatile knife! Ulu have been found in a range of sizes, with blades measuring up to 8" long, depending on the intended application. Ulu intended for precise work have blades measuring around 2" long. As you might guess based on their crescent shape, they are used in a rocking motion. The earliest versions were made of stone. A common use now is to chop vegetables and prepare foods for cooking. I've read about folks in modern day America who swear by their ulu, even claiming that they've replaced their "standard" chef's knives due to their versatility and ease of use. Something to think about.

CHAPTER 2

HUNTING KNIVES

Though it's no surprise to anyone that many knives are for the kitchen, anybody who either hunts or knows a hunter can tell you that the variety of hunting knives available is just as numerous. This diverse chapter includes a Drop Point Knife (page 63), Drop Point Hunter's Knife (page 73), Semi-Skinner Knife (page 81), Skinner Knife (page 91), and Mini Hunter Fixed Blade (page 101). Field dressing and preparing your hunted game will be more enjoyable using these sturdy fixed blades with chunky handles you've made yourself.

DROP POINT KNIFE

A splash of figure for a go-to knife in the field

MATERIALS & TOOLS

> Drop point knife kit
> Wood of choice
> Tablesaw
> Clamp
> Pencil or marker
> Jigsaw
> Epoxy
> Drill press
> Drill bit, ¼"
> Belt sander
> Rat tail file
> Wood finish of choice

A drop point knife is used for various butchering tasks like cutting, skinning, and carving. This is the first of several projects in the book that use stabilized wood blanks, which is great to work with and offers a few possibilities that aren't possible with traditional lumber. For more on stabilized lumber, see the box on page 79. I had a few stabilized blanks dyed in bold colors, which was fun, but I chose this blank for the opposite reason—it's definitely eye-catching, but the colors are all natural. I think it makes for a really beautiful knife.

— 1 —

Rip the blank into two parts. Use a bandsaw—or even a handsaw, if you want to go old-school—to rip the handle blank into two pieces.

— 2 —

Ready the epoxy. Mix up a small batch of 5-minute epoxy to attach the first side of the handle to the knife blank.

— 3 —

Secure the first side. Clamp the blank onto the handle. To avoid gluing the blank to your work surface, clean up any squeeze-out quickly using lacquer thinner.

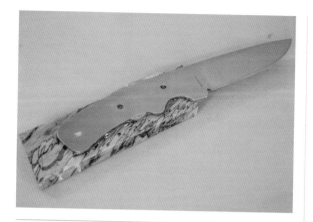

— 4 —

Check your work. Even though you're using 5-minute epoxy, it's best to wait 30 minutes or so before handling the workpiece. Here it is, freshly unclamped.

— 5 —

Rough-cut the handle. Use a jigsaw to remove the excess stock around the handle. A scrollsaw or bandsaw would work as well.

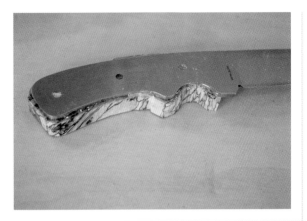

— 6 —

Take it slowly. When using a jigsaw to cut the blank to shape, be sure not to cut into the metal itself—you can easily trim down to the metal with a belt sander later.

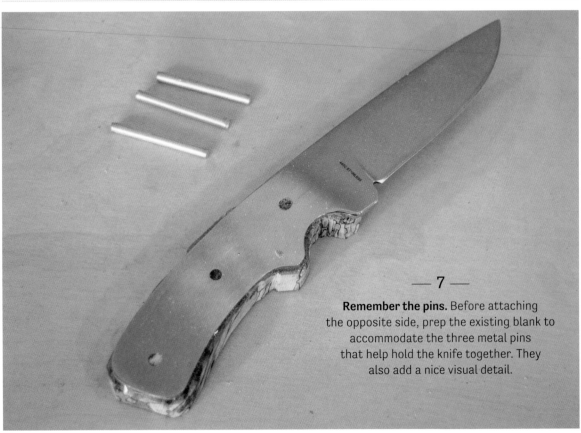

— 7 —

Remember the pins. Before attaching the opposite side, prep the existing blank to accommodate the three metal pins that help hold the knife together. They also add a nice visual detail.

— 8 —

Drill for the pins. If you glued on the other piece of wood, the location of the holes would be gone forever. Instead, use the metal knife blank as a guide for drilling through the metal holes, then through the handle blank.

— 9 —

Keep everything in its place. Here's a shot of the exterior, roughed out, and with holes drilled. Notice that using a drill press insures that the holes are aligned and perpendicular to the blade.

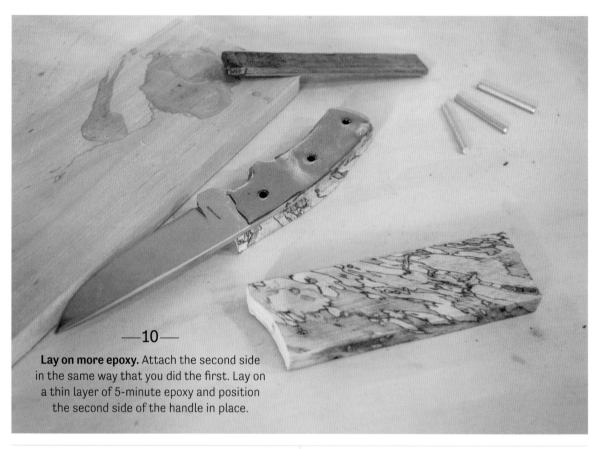

—10—

Lay on more epoxy. Attach the second side in the same way that you did the first. Lay on a thin layer of 5-minute epoxy and position the second side of the handle in place.

—11—

Clamp it in place. Pressure from a single clamp is all it takes to hold the handle together until the epoxy cures.

—12—

Head back to the drill press. Use the holes already drilled in the first side of the handle as a guide for drilling through the second side of the handle.

—13—

Saw away the waste. Put the jigsaw back into play to rough out the contours on the second side of the handle.

—14—

Set the pins. The pins are easy to install—simply add a little epoxy in the holes, then pound the pins flush (or close to it) with a hammer. It's satisfying work. These pins were pretty long: no biggie, though. Just use a hacksaw or rotary cutter to nip them off, or simply use an aggressive sanding belt to grind them away.

—15—

Shape the handle. While the belt sander is best for shaping the handle (as shown on page 71), some nooks are simply too tight for a belt sander. In this case it was easier to shape the handle using a rat tail file. You could also use a small sanding drum chucked in a drill press or an oscillating spindle sander.

—16—

It takes a village (of tools). There are a number of other low-tech handtools that could work for getting into the tight nooks and crannies: rasps, chisels, and files all come in handy when shaping handles.

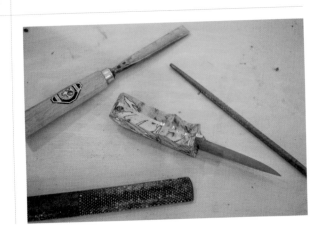

GET CREATIVE WITH A BELT SANDER

The belt sander is a surprisingly versatile tool when it comes to working on knife handles. Not only can it flatten large areas quickly, it can even get into small, tight spots. I also like it for easing the edges of handles and creating contours. Experiment with holding the workpiece at an angle, and you'll see new opportunities to create interesting shapes and styles. If you have a lot of material to remove, I recommend 24- or 36-grit belts. 50 or 60 grit is about right for general shaping. Use 80 or 120 grit for finer work, then switch to a random orbit sander or hand-sanding after that.

Before firing up the sander, cleaning the belt makes a big difference in efficiency and the life of the abrasives. The freshly cleaned belt (36 grit) flattens the wood in no time.

Start with the handle flat on the worktable to ensure that the handle remains perpendicular as you sand it down to the metal.

The tight ends of the sander come in handy for shaping tighter curved surfaces on the handle.

Holding the handle at an angle allows you to knock off the hard edges. With a steady hand, you can even shape consistent and refined roundovers.

DROP POINT HUNTER'S KNIFE

A sculpted handle worth a second look

MATERIALS & TOOLS

> Drop point hunter's knife kit
> Wood of choice
> Tablesaw
> Jointer
> Planer
> Spring clamps (2)
> Pencil or marker
> Bandsaw
> Epoxy
> Drill press
> Drill bit, ⁵⁄₁₆"
> Drill bit, ¹³⁄₁₆"
> Belt sander
> Random-orbit sander
> Wood finish of choice

Drop point knives are a hunter's go-to in the field. So you want a handle that is comfortable and will stand up to long lengths of hard work. While I love to use up hardwood scraps that come from my shop as knife handles, this green, spalted, stabilized tamarind really caught my eye. It has a fun color overall and has a lot of cool detail in the spalted figure. But if green isn't your thing, that's OK—similar stabilized blanks are available in a variety of colors. For more on stabilized woods, check out the sidebar on page 79.

— 1 —

Start with the kit. This kit comes with a one-piece knife blank and three threaded barrel bolt–style fasteners. Once the fasteners have been pulled out, you can see how they go together.

— 2 —

The Incredible Hulk strikes again! Well, it only appears so. Rip the handle in half at the tablesaw. The green dust shown here is a good reminder of the importance of protecting yourself—a dust mask is highly recommended when sanding spalted material.

— 3 —

Attach the first side. You can approach this process in a couple of different ways. Here the first side of the handle is attached to the blade blank using 5-minute epoxy and a couple of spring clamps prior to shaping the handle.

— 4 —

Saw it out. After the epoxy dries, use a bandsaw or jigsaw to trim away the excess stock. Make sure not to hit the metal and dull your blade.

— 5 —

Inspect your work. Don't try to cut away everything—just trim as close as you can without touching the metal, knowing that you can sand away the rest later.

— 6 —

Drill for the barrel bolts. To transfer the hole locations to the exterior of the knife handle, drill through the wood with your drill press.

— 7 —

Add the other side. Glue on the other side of the handle using 5-minute epoxy and a few spring clamps to secure it in place.

— 8 —

Shape the second side.
Once the epoxy is dry on side number two, use the bandsaw to cut away the excess wood.

— 9 —

Sand creatively. The rounded end of a stationary belt sander makes quick work of the scalloped concave curves on the handle blank.

—10—

Countersink for the barrel bolts. The barrel bolts need to be countersunk on each side. How much depends on the thickness of your handle. At the drill press, make shallow cuts and test the fit frequently until they fit. And take it slow. If you go too far the barrel bolts won't tighten all the way.

—11—

Install the barrel bolts. To secure the bolts, just use a small Allen wrench. No adhesive is required.

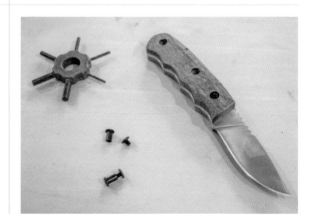

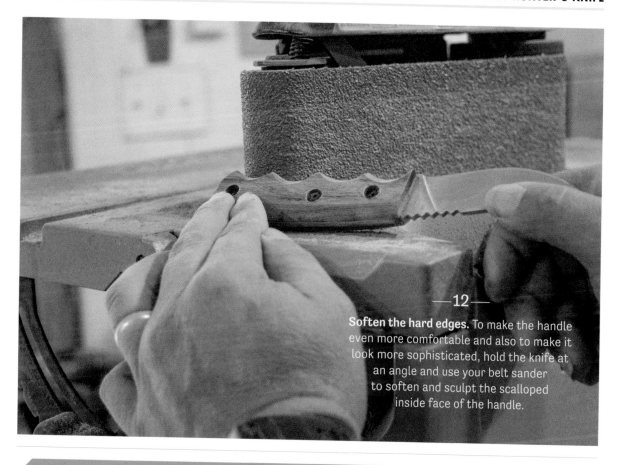

—12—

Soften the hard edges. To make the handle even more comfortable and also to make it look more sophisticated, hold the knife at an angle and use your belt sander to soften and sculpt the scalloped inside face of the handle.

WHAT IS STABILIZED WOOD?

Stabilized wood is a product created by a nifty fusion of nature and science. It involves a process where clear resin mixed with colored dye is injected into the wood cells under pressure. This eliminates checking or cracking and makes the wood water resistant. All good attributes for knife handles to have!

And they don't always use colored dye—plenty of natural-looking woods are available too. Stabilized wood blanks have been custom cut and meticulously selected for their beautiful and unpredictable grain patterns and interesting colors, such as spalted woods, for example.

SEMI-SKINNER KNIFE

A light knife for hunting

MATERIALS & TOOLS

> Semi-skinner kit
> Scales or wood of choice about ⅛" x 1½" x 4½"
> Tablesaw
> Miter saw
> Epoxy
> Spring clamps
> Drill press with ⁵⁄₃₂" bit
> Jigsaw
> Hammer
> Belt sander
> Random-orbit sander
> Finish of choice

Knives used for skinning are typically short and designed to cut through hide without tearing muscle or tissue. For this blade I chose ash becasue it is super-dense and durable. There's nothing tricky about this creating and installing this handle—and the knife blank has an extra hole at the bottom where you can add a leather loop to hang the knife for storage or display.

— 1 —

Prep the parts. Begin by ripping a strip of ash about 12" long x 5/16" thick.

— 2 —

Apply epoxy to one side. Crosscut the strip in half using a miter saw to product two equal halves. Then spread 5-minute epoxy onto one side of the knife.

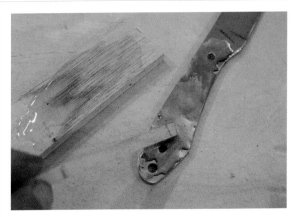

— 3 —

Clamp up the first side. A pair of spring clamps hold the ash in place and apply plenty of pressure.

— 4 —

Drill the pin holes. Once the epoxy has dried—allow 30 minutes—head to the drill press to drill the holes in the wood. If you choose to use the extra hole on the end, this is the time to drill it.

— 5 —

Check out your progress. Here's what the knife and handle should look like at this point. Next, it's time to remove the excess wood.

— 6 —

Clean up the waste. Depending on what tools you have available, you could use a bandsaw, coping saw, or jigsaw to trim away the excess wood. No need to worry about removing every bit of waste—you can use more refined tools for that.

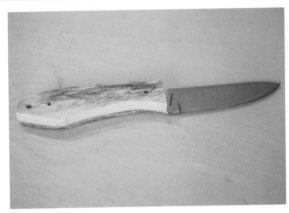

— 7 —

Continue removing wood. Files, rasps, and sandpaper come in handy for removing the excess wood. Aim for a handle that is flush with the metal tang on the blade.

— 8 —

Attach the second half of the handle. Once the first side is cleaned up, glue on the second side with 5-minute epoxy. Again, spring clamps offer plenty of holding power.

— 9 —

Drill through the holes. To finish drilling the holes, head back to the drill press and run the bit through the holes that you started earlier.

—10—

Clean up the second half. To safely use the jigsaw to shape the other half of the handle, clamp the knife to the edge of your bench, making sure to protect the blade from by wrapping it in multiple layers of paper towel. Even though this is a short knife, it's long enough to clamp down and allow enough room to maneuver the jigsaw.

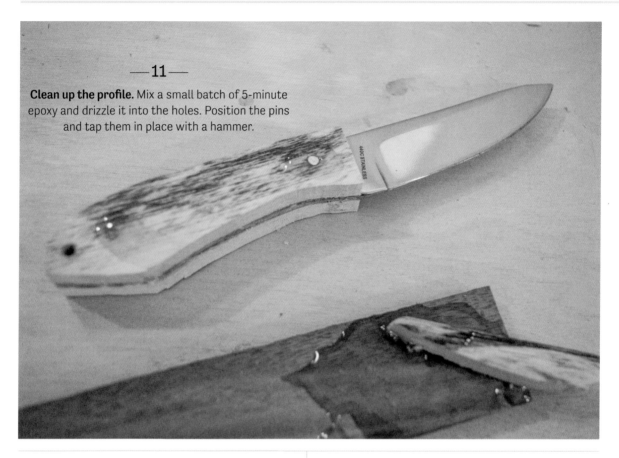

—11—

Clean up the profile. Mix a small batch of 5-minute epoxy and drizzle it into the holes. Position the pins and tap them in place with a hammer.

—12—

Flatten the back first. The recommended sanding sequence is to flatten the back first with a belt sander. Then proceed "around the horn" at the bottom of the knife to reveal the exact shape there. Then transition into the curvier, more complex portion on the front of the knife.

—13—

Review your work. With many designs there is a nook at the top edge of the front of the handle that the sander can't reach, but this knife design doesn't have that. As you can see, the big curve on the front of the handle is smooth at the top (just below the logo stamped into the steel), and this makes the sanding a breeze. No hand-sanding, chiseling, or filing required.

—14—

Smooth the concave areas. The curve at the end of the sanding belt is surprisingly versatile for sanding concave bits on knife handles.

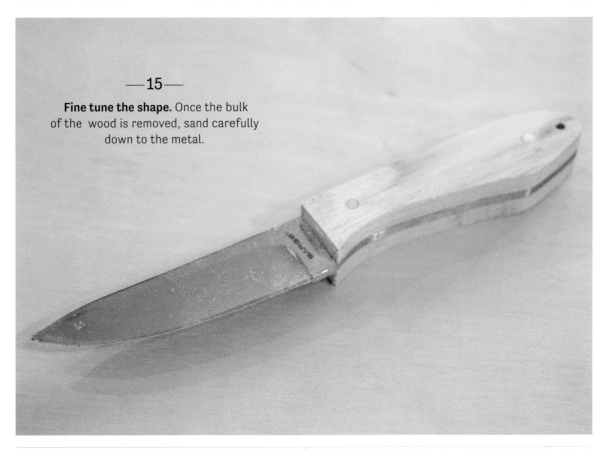

—15—

Fine tune the shape. Once the bulk of the wood is removed, sand carefully down to the metal.

—16—

Finish shaping. To ease the edges of the handle, use a random-orbit sander. Then sand all surfaces to 220 grit by hand and apply your finish of choice. For more on finishing, see the box on page 89.

YOU'RE NOT FINISHED UNTIL YOU FINISH

Do knife handles need to be finished? Not necessarily, but most of the handles in this book will be subjected to wet or sloppy conditions, and applying a finish offers protection against stains. There's also the aspect of looks—I think we all recognize that finish really makes wood grain "pop." Every time I teach a class on this, people can't wait to apply the finish. They've spent hours making a handle that looks relatively dull, but adding that finish changes the look entirely—not to mention spalted and figured woods really benefit from a couple coats of varnish. In my opinion, the best finish for knife handles is oil-based poly.

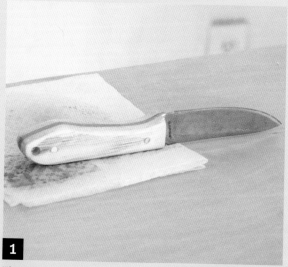

1 There's no need to get fancy with the application process. Simply wipe on the first coat of varnish using a folded paper towel.

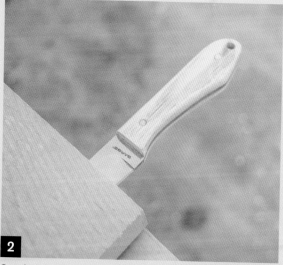

2 Sandwich the blade between the edge of the bench and some kind of heavy object while the varnish dries. Sand using 220-grit sandpaper between coats. Three to four coats is pretty typical.

SKINNER KNIFE

A straightforward design goes together quickly

MATERIALS & TOOLS

> Skinner knife kit
> Wood of choice
> Tablesaw
> Jointer
> Planer
> Spring clamps (2)
> Pencil or marker
> Bandsaw
> Epoxy
> Drill press
> Drill bit, ¼"
> Belt sander
> Allen wrench
> Wood finish of choice

This skinner is a beefy knife, and right away I knew that I wanted to pair it with a rich cherry handle. Cherry develops such rich, deep color as it ages and I felt it was a perfect choice to go with a knife that somebody would have and use for years and years. I was thrilled with the result—it was a very classic look, indeed.

— 1 —

Start with the basics. The block of cherry used here has a few inclusions (the thin black lines that run with the grain) that add a little character. Sometimes the little details make all the difference.

— 2 —

Clean up the handle blank. If your stock is rough-sawn, a couple of quick passes on the jointer are essential to establish a flat, smooth face.

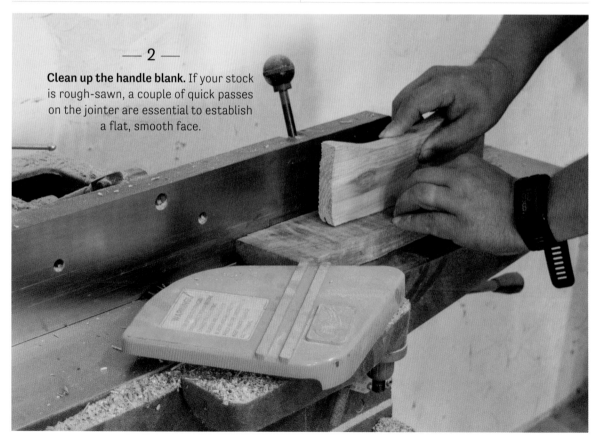

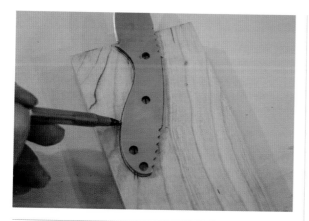

— 3 —

Trace the shape. Position the blade on the handle blank with an eye toward choosing a grain pattern that works well with the handle shape.

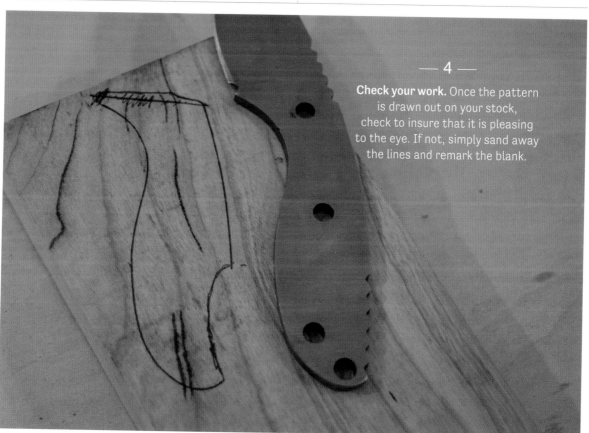

— 4 —

Check your work. Once the pattern is drawn out on your stock, check to insure that it is pleasing to the eye. If not, simply sand away the lines and remark the blank.

— 5 —

Saw out the handle blanks. At the bandsaw, cut the profile to rough shape—leaving it large enough to handle comfortably when held on edge—and then rip down the center to create a blank for each side of the blade.

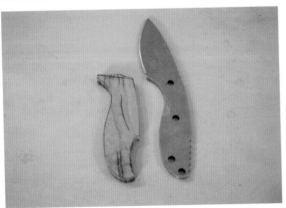

— 6 —

Double-check the first side. Once cut, set the handle stock into position on the blade and make sure there is a slight overhang on all sides.

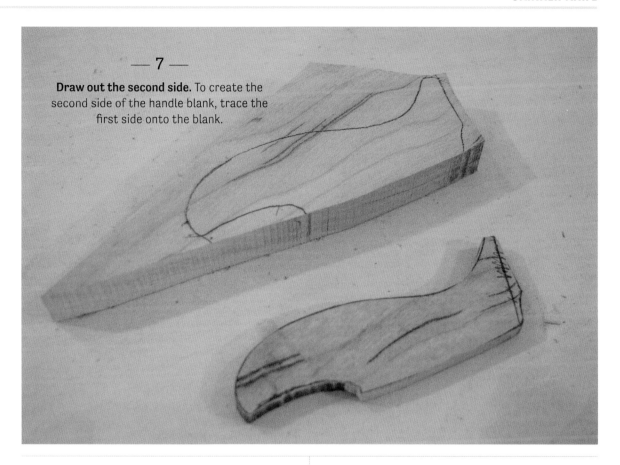

— 7 —

Draw out the second side. To create the second side of the handle blank, trace the first side onto the blank.

— 8 —

You're ready to go. After bandsawing the second side to thickness and cutting its profile, your three main components are ready for glue up.

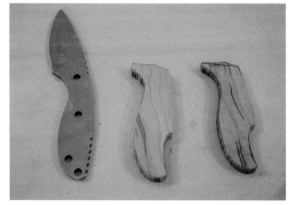

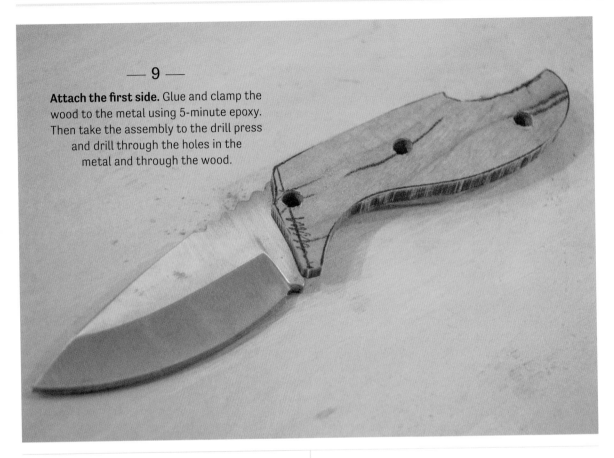

— 9 —

Attach the first side. Glue and clamp the wood to the metal using 5-minute epoxy. Then take the assembly to the drill press and drill through the holes in the metal and through the wood.

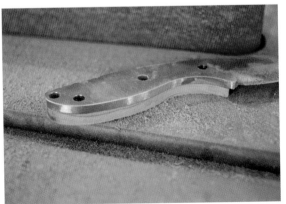

—10—

Shape the first side. A belt sander makes it easy to remove the excess wood that overhangs the metal on the handle.

—11—

Glue on the second side. Attach the other half of the handle as you did the first—lay on a thin layer of epoxy and then use a few spring clamps to secure it in place.

—12—

Sand it to shape. With the handle fully assembled and the epoxy dry, even up the wood on the other half of the knife. Using a belt sander makes quick work sanding the wood flush to the metal.

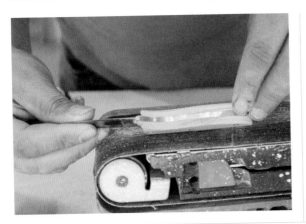

—13—

Soften the edges. Once the profile is cleaned up, hold the knife at an angle to ease the edges and round the transitions in a more contoured way.

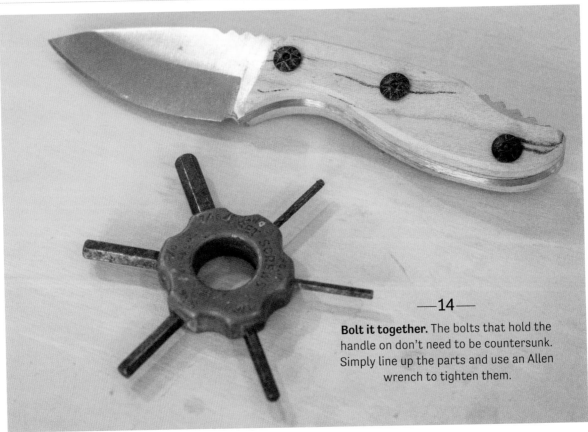

—14—

Bolt it together. The bolts that hold the handle on don't need to be countersunk. Simply line up the parts and use an Allen wrench to tighten them.

HANDLE SHAPING BASICS

The goal—especially for a small, unusually shaped knife like this—is to fashion a handle that feels smooth, organic, and doesn't have any awkward angles or flat surfaces. Keep three things in mind:

Work slowly. You can't get into much trouble if you slow down and nibble away at it. Rushing can cause you to take off too much material or cause an injury.

Have a plan. Approach knife handles in a systematic fashion. Begin by flattening the areas that need it. Clean up the handle profile so that no excess remains. Last, ease the edges and contours by holding or moving the knife at an angle relative to the sanding belt.

Focus on symmetry. To achieve a symmetrical result, employ a symmetrical process. You should literally think, "Make three passes on this side. Now three passes on the other." And so on. Never try to make a complete right side, for example, and then hope to match the other side after the fact. Is it possible? Sure, but it's certainly the hard way to go at it.

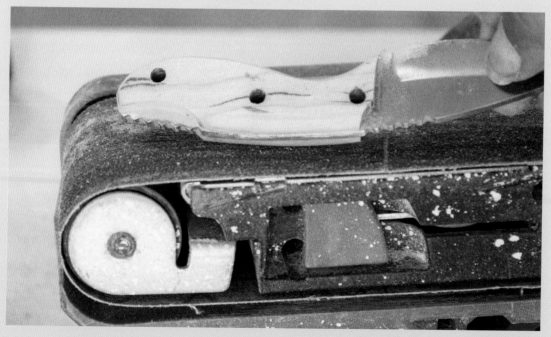

MINI HUNTER FIXED BLADE

A one-of-a-kind handle made from an antler

MATERIALS & TOOLS

> Mini hunter fixed blade knife kit
> Wood of choice
> Spring clamps (2)
> Pencil or marker
> Bandsaw
> Epoxy
> Drill press
> Drill bit to match pins
> Belt sander
> Wood finish of choice

Not surprisingly, hunting knives have evolved over time as materials have improved and designs have been tweaked to reflect the practical needs of people seeking to dress game in the field. Compact drop point knives like this one allow one to work precisely in small spaces, and the 440c steel blade represents the state of the art in bladesmithing. 440 steel is common in knife-making (all 440 steels are stainless, which makes cleaning the blade a snap), but only 440c offers the best combination of durability and the ability to take a really sharp edge. This mini hunter will be a fine addition to any hunter's kit.

WORKING WITH ANTLERS

Antlers? Yes—easy to find and easy to work with. Once cleaned up and shaped to fit, an antler makes an attractive and durable handle with an all-natural look. I also love the traditional feel; antlers have been used for knife handles for eons. Once I had committed to the idea, my only question was where to get a piece of antler. I stumbled across some at the grocery store near the dog food for dogs to chew on, and the low price tag seemed almost too good to be true. Make sure you grab a piece that is large enough for your knife's handle.

— 1 —

Mark a centerline. Use a pencil to mark out a centerline along the section of antler you plan to use for the handle. This centerline will separate the two sides of the handle.

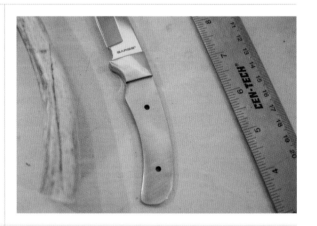

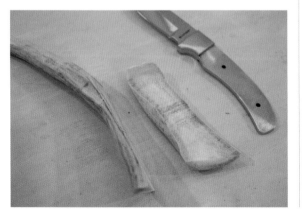

— 2 —

Aim for a straight cut. At the bandsaw, cut along your centerline to separate the antler into the two sides of the handle. The bandsaw won't make a perfectly smooth or flat cut, but a steady cut rate should yield good results.

— 3 —

Clean up the cut. To flatten and smooth the surfaces created by your bandsaw cut, hold the inside faces of the handle blanks flat against the belt sander. Then sand a straight line where the handle blank meets the bolster on the blade.

— 4 —

Attach the first half. Mix up a small batch of 5-minute epoxy and lay a thin layer onto the inside face of the antler. Then secure it in place with two spring clamps. Make sure that the antler overhangs the metal on all sides.

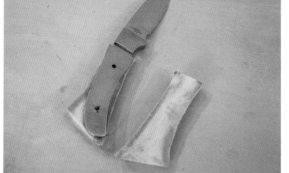

— 5 —

Line up the second side. Test the fit of the second side against the handle section on the blade and use your belt sander to create a flat edge where the end of the antler handle abuts the bolster on the blade blank.

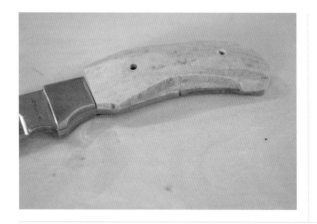

— 6 —

Shape the handle. At the drill press, drill through the holes in the blade itself and into the antler. To get a better look at the exact profile of the metal handle, begin removing the extra material with your bandsaw.

— 7 —

Sand it to shape. A belt sander is perfect for fine-tuning the fit of the parts and sanding the antler flush to the handle section of the blade.

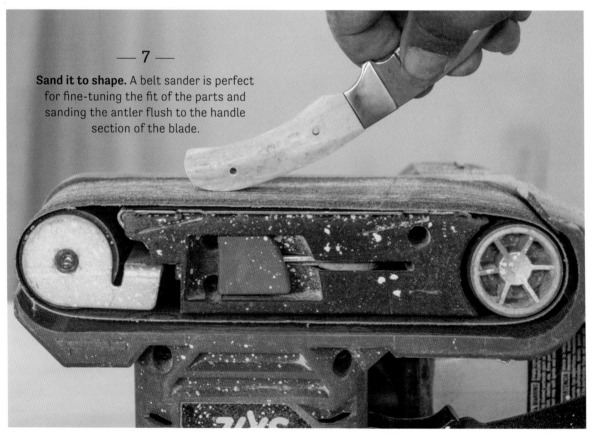

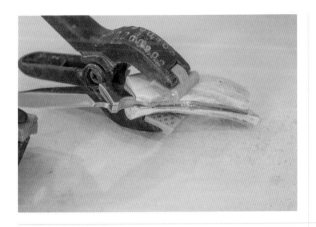

— 8 —

Attach the second side. Just as you did with the first side, mix up a small batch of 5-minute epoxy and secure the second side of the handle to the blade. Use a spring clamp to hold it all together while the epoxy cures.

— 9 —

Saw off the excess. When the epoxy dries, use the bandsaw to trim the excess from the second half of the handle.

—10—

Use the first side as a guide. Having already cleaned up the first half of the handle makes it much easier to see what material needs to be sawn away.

—11—

Sand down to the metal. Fine-tuning the fit goes quickly with a belt sander. Be careful to only remove material from the profile of the knife and not the outside faces of the handle. Otherwise, you'll lose the natural look of the antler.

—12—

Drill it out. Back at the drill press, drill through the holes on the first side to create the holes on the second side. Because you're drilling directly through the holes already established, the holes on the second side automatically align.

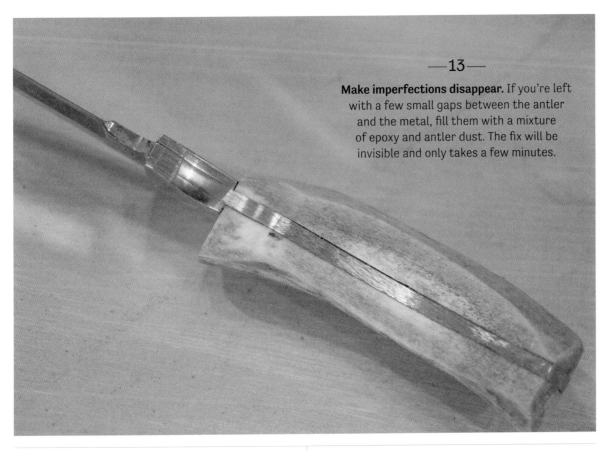

—13—

Make imperfections disappear. If you're left with a few small gaps between the antler and the metal, fill them with a mixture of epoxy and antler dust. The fix will be invisible and only takes a few minutes.

—14—

Install the pins. Setting the pins into place is easy. Simply install the female end in place on one side and the male end in place on the other. Then use a vise or a small screw clamp to tighten them down and lock them into place.

CHAPTER 3

FOLDING KNIVES

Folding knives require a bit of special treatment. The kits are a bit more complex versus a fixed blade due to the moving parts, but aren't as scary as you might think. After working through the process for the Pocket Knife (page 111) and the Small Custom Folding Knife (page 117), you'll have a great foundation for branching out into other folding knife kits. These projects are also great for keeping in a pocket for when you need a knife on the go.

POCKET KNIFE

A clean design as simple as it looks

MATERIALS & TOOLS

> - Custom folding knife kit
> - Scales or wood of choice about 5" x 1½" x ³⁄₁₆"
> - Pencil
> - Painter's tape
> - Bandsaw
> - Epoxy
> - Spring clamps
> - Belt sander
> - Sanding drum in drill press, spindle sander, or belt sander
> - Random-orbit sander

When I first looked at this kit, I was a little bit daunted. It seemed so much more complicated than the others I'd seen. But once I took a good look, I discovered that not only was it quite simple; it was in fact easier than most of the others. Instead of having to attach the handle scales to a knife blank with metal pins or fasteners, the two handle scales are simply glued down. The only remaining challenge—and it's not a bad one at all—is to sculpt the top end of the scales to be flush with the profile of the metal on the end of the knife where they meet. It felt like I was unlocking a mystery—and in this case, the prize was a great-looking pocket knife.

— 1 —

Trace the handle shape. If possible, select scales that are already the right thickness (close to 3/16"). That means there's no milling required. If not, mill them to the correct thickness. Trace the handle onto one of them and then tape the two halves together.

— 2 —

Start cutting out the handle. Begin cutting along the pencil line. A bandsaw is definitely the tool for the job, although a scrollsaw would work great too.

— 3 —

Continue removing waste. Make any removal cuts, like these, in stages. Use a series of relief cuts to avoid taking any corners too tightly and stressing the blade (or yourself).

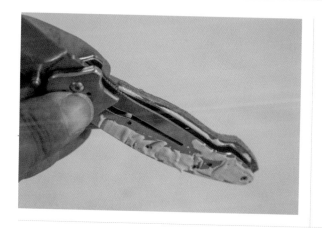

— 4 —

Glue on the handles. Though the scales are the same, they aren't attached the same way. One side of the knife is "fixed" and the other has the blade lock attached to it. Glue on the fixed side first; after it dries, glue on the other side. You can see that the epoxy does not cover the entire area on the non-fixed side—make sure not to glue the blade lock in place. This is very important.

— 5 —

Clamp the handle. Simple spring clamps provide lots of pressure on the handle—two is all you need. You can also clamp the knife itself to your workbench to work on it easily.

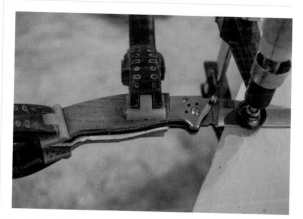

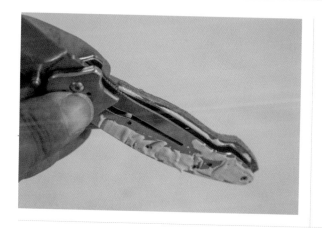

— 6 —

Sand the handle. Once the epoxy is dry, the excess wood can be sanded off using whatever tools you like. A belt sander works well (see page 71).

— 7 —

Make sure the blade lock is free. This view shows how the blade lock is free to move around as need be.

— 8 —

Sand the handle contours. To sand the contours on the front face of this knife, use sanding drums in a drill press, an oscillating spindle sander, or the radius end of a belt sander.

— 9 —

Continue sanding. Remember the mention earlier about sanding the wood flush where it meets the steel on the end (page 113)? Yup, this is it. It isn't hard to do, but the challenge is to not butcher the steel along the way. You could cover the steel with a layer of masking tape—not a bad idea—but it is also useful to be able to see and feel as you go.

—10—

Sand down the handle thickness.
Use a random-orbit sander to buzz down the wood, working slowly and conservatively. In the end, the steel and the wood should be at the same level so the whole thing looks just right.

GOOD OLD-FASHIONED WHITTLING

I vividly remember getting my first pocket knife as a kid. I imagine a lot of people do! In fact, I remember the early days of my "collection" of three pocket knives, and how impressed I was with myself at the time. Beyond their value as a source of pride, what exactly did I do with them? Well, I remember whittling, that's for sure. My first efforts focused on carving sharp tips on "arrows" that I crudely fashioned from willow branches to accompany my equally crude homemade bow. In the decades since, I haven't exactly become a master carver, but I have found another nice use for a pocket knife. I've become somewhat obsessed with carving wooden spoons, and a pocket knife is a great tool for shaping the handle and the backside of the spoon's bowl. My first knives somehow got lost in the shuffle somewhere along the way, but I've got new knives now, and I'm glad to be able to carry on the humble tradition of whittling in one way or another.

SMALL CUSTOM FOLDING KNIFE

A petite knife for any pocket

MATERIALS & TOOLS

›   Small custom folding knife kit with 2" blade
›   Scales or wood of choice about ⅛" x ¾" x 3" .
›   Painter's tape
›   Pen
›   Bandsaw, scrollsaw, or jigsaw
›   Drill press
›   Drill bit, ³⁄₁₆"
›   Countersink bit
›   Epoxy
›   Spring clamps
›   Sanding drum in drill press, spindle sander, or belt sander
›   Torx wrench (included with kit)
›   Finish of choice

Talk about life's little ironies: prior to making a handle for the other folding knife in this book, I was a little intimidated. When I actually went for it, though, I discovered that it was really straightforward. What a relief. I assumed, then, that this knife would also be a bit of a walk in the park. Au contraire; this one kicked me right in the seat of the pants. While the other one came fully assembled, this one did not. It also came with some really convoluted instructions. But fear not, dear reader—that's what I'm here for. Here is a straightforward approach that will make for a much easier and more satisfying process. And the result really is worth it—this little knife is a gem indeed.

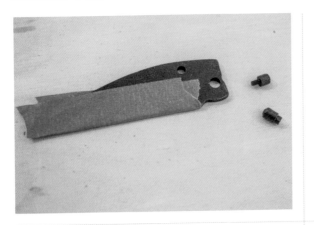

— 1 —

Apply tape to the sharp edge. Tape up the blade with a few layers of painter's tape. Even if you don't usually do this, consider that this blade is small, harder to work with, and therefore a bit more of a risk.

— 2 —

Trace the fixed side. Because this is a folding knife with a lock, it has a fixed side and a locking (moving) side. The fixed side can be used as a pattern to create the knife scales. You'll need two. They don't need to be mirror images of each other, although you could do it that way and designate a "right" and "left" side.

3

Cut out the handles. You could use a bandsaw, scrollsaw, or jigsaw to cut out the scales.

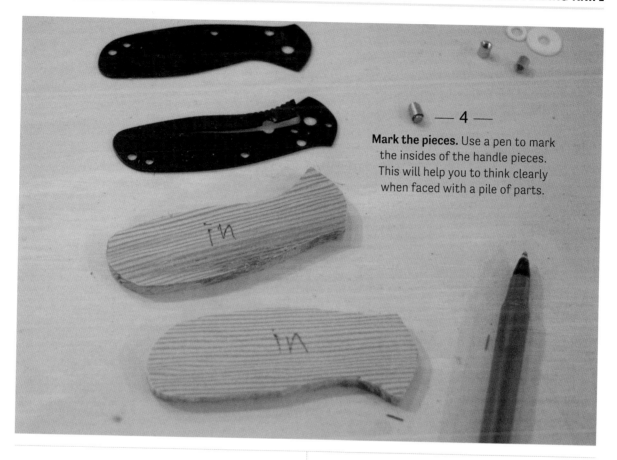

— 4 —

Mark the pieces. Use a pen to mark the insides of the handle pieces. This will help you to think clearly when faced with a pile of parts.

— 5 —

Mark holes. You need to mark three holes on each half—a large diameter one for the pivot bolt that holds the blade, and two smaller holes for screws that attach the two sides to each other. The optional hole at the far left is for a key chain (omitted in the photos).

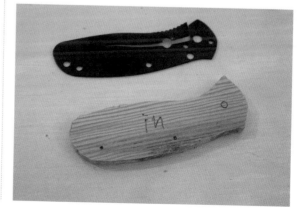

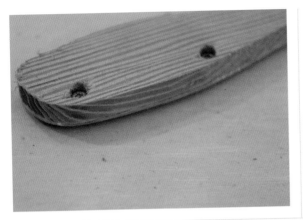

— 6 —

Drill and countersink the holes. After drilling the small holes for the screws, you'll need to countersink them enough for the screws to protrude into the inside of the knife.

— 7 —

Attach the handle and begin sanding. Glue the wood to the metal and allow to dry. Clean up the excess wood with whatever sanding device works best for you.

— 8 —

Check the parts. Here's a good look at the interior of the knife. The four screws (two per side) that fit into the countersunk holes fit into a pair of threaded bushings. This is what holds the knife together, in addition to the pivot bolt that holds the blade.

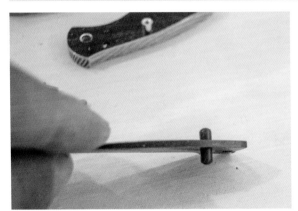

— 9 —

Place the blade rod. A small metal threaded rod fits into the end of the blade. This keeps it from falling too far into the interior of the knife.

—10—

Insert the pivot bolt. Assembly is coming along: the large diameter bolt is the pivot bolt. You can get a feel for the way the two sides will sandwich together.

—11—

Install the small washer. Before inserting the blade, attach the small white washer provided with the kit.

—12—

Install the large washer. Position the blade. The large white washer goes on the other side, and the silver barrel-shaped spacer goes in the hole just below it. It doesn't protrude down into the wood, so you won't need to drill for it to fit.

—13—

Assemble and apply finish. The wrench included with the kit is all you need to finish tightening the connections. Not as complicated as it seemed to start with! Apply desired finish.

POCKET KNIFE HISTORY

Unsurprisingly, the first pocket knife I ever saw belonged to my dad. He had a classic Barlow folding knife that I still can picture clearly in my mind. In the writing of this book, though, I started to wonder a bit about the history of the pocket knife, and just how far back it went. Here's what I learned.

The oldest pocket knife yet discovered dates back to 500 to 600 BC in what is now the country of Austria. It has a metal blade and bone handle. Many pocket knives have been found throughout portions of the former Roman Empire. Interestingly, they belong to a class of "friction folders," in which the blade pivots freely and the person holding the blade needed to squeeze the handle to keep the blade from folding back in. Fortunately we've seen lots of improvements in this department since then. An especially interesting knife from the Roman era was likely made for a very wealthy person: it was made from silver instead of bronze, and it features a spoon and fork. This makes it pretty much the earliest known iteration of the famous Swiss Army knife. Many pocket knives from the Viking era have been found, and many of them utilize a small clasp to keep the blades open. Around 1650, the peasant knife (or "penny knife") began to be produced at a large scale, and it was affordable to the masses. It had a wooden handle and is the most recognizable relative to today's pocket knives.

CHAPTER 4

MORE COOL PROJECTS

This chapter has all the cool projects that just didn't quite fit into the other chapters. You'll wonder how you survived without the Camp Hatchet (page 127)—a useful gift for anyone who likes to spend time in the great outdoors. A Desk Knife (page 135) is a fantastic way to make sure your knife-making hobby gets into yet another room in your house, and makes mail opening a breeze. Last but not least, you'll get a lot of mileage out of the Bottle Opener (page 145) that not only cracks open bottles with ease, but shucks oysters and chips ice too.

CAMP HATCHET

A handy little camping axe

MATERIALS & TOOLS

› Hatchet kit
› Scales or wood of choice 5" x 1½" x ⅜" (we used Fiji Onyx 2-piece knife scales #K10-510)
› Torx wrench (including in the kit)
› Pencil or marker
› Epoxy
› Spring clamps (2)
› Screw clamp
› Paper towels
› Router with guide bushing, ½" flush-trimming bit, and round-over bit
› Drill press
› Drill bit, ¼"
› Drill bit, ¹¹/₃₂"
› Painter's tape
› Belt sander
› Wood finish of choice

I love this hatchet so much that I see myself making a few more as gifts for friends. It is small enough to pack right up and take backpacking, yet beefy enough to be a total workhorse around the campsite or just the backyard. It is made of super-thick (roughly ¼") steel and is plenty long to lend the leverage you need. I might just have to start looking around the shop and setting aside material for future handles after all.

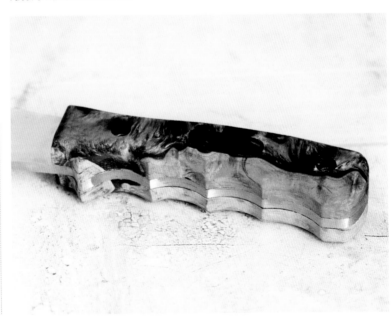

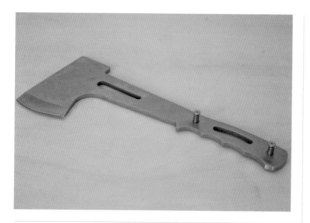

— 1 —

Look over the design. The design of this hatchet is just gorgeous. The little cutout in the middle helps to provide a tough, industrial feel. Because of the heavy use that this hatchet is designed for, the scales will attach to the hatchet with a pair of stout fasteners—more on this later.

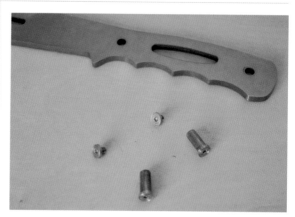

— 2 —

Make sure you have the fasteners. The fasteners are easy to work with—they come apart and go back together with a Torx wrench that is included with the kit.

— 3 —

Select the scale material. A fairly dramatic set of pre-made scales offers some interesting contrast for this project.

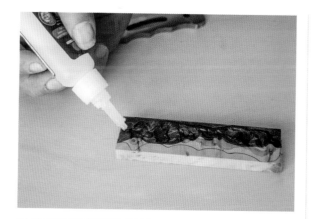

— 4 —

Glue on the first scale. This set of scales came ready-to-use, but that's not always the case—sometimes you're buying a single, solid block that you'll need to mill down. Either way, trace the handle placement and then glue on the first scale. Five-minute epoxy works very well to bond the scales with the steel (see sidebar on page 133).

— 5 —

Remove excess wood. Because of the hatchet's size, you can try some new techniques. For example, clamp it to the edge of your workbench and use a router with a guide bushing to remove the excess material. (Note the photo does not show correct positioning for the router. The router should run along the top with the bearing near the ground, not the ceiling.)

— 6 —

Continue removing excess. The scalloped handle of the hatchet is perfectly shaped to allow the router bit access. No additional sanding should be needed.

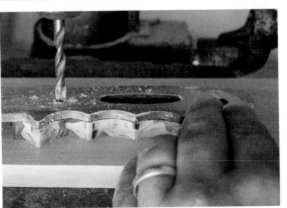

— 7 —

Drill the first half of the pin holes. Use a drill press to carry the holes past the steel and through the wood.

— 8 —

Drill the center recess. To create the center recess in the scales, use a $7/16"$ drill bit to create a starter hole. Use a screw clamp to hold the hatchet on your workbench. Plunge your router bit into it and allow the bearing to ride on the steel and hog away the excess material.

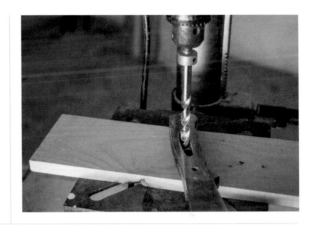

— 9 —

Attach and drill the second scale. After gluing on the second scale, drill the holes the rest of the way through and use a slightly wider diameter bit to countersink the flanged ends of the fasteners. This is easy to do, but you'll want to go just a little at a time so you don't overdo it. It helps to mark the depth on the drill bit with some painter's tape.

—10—

Remove excess wood. The router setup works perfectly on the other side of the handle as well.

—11—

Drill through the center hole. To finish off the cut-out in the handle, bore a hole all the way through as you did before.

—12—

Complete the center hole. Flip the hatchet over and fire up the router. As you can see, there isn't a ton of bearing surface for the base to ride on, but it's enough. Go slowly and carefully and you'll be fine.

—13—

Shape the handle. Mount a roundover bit in the router chuck and shape the edges of the handle. Very little sanding is required when using the router.

—14—

Sand off any milling marks. As usual, a power sander makes quick work of things when it comes to removing burn marks or milling marks.

EPOXY IS THE ADHESIVE OF CHOICE

Adhering scales to metal for knives—or in this case, a hatchet—is pretty easy. All you need is the right glue for the job, which, for me, is 5-minute epoxy. While some use polyurethane glue, I don't like the accompanying squeeze-out that creates an unnecessary mess to clean up later.

Once, in a pickle and trying the save myself the short ride to the hardware store to buy epoxy, I tried cyanoacrylate. At first, it seemed like it might hold, but it eventually loosened, so I sanded both surfaces and made the dreaded drive to the hardware store. Some things, like epoxy, work so well there's no need to innovate.

I tried out cyanoacrylate on this project.

DESK KNIFE

Open your mail with style

MATERIALS & TOOLS

› Desk knife kit
› Wood of choice
› Tablesaw
› Jointer
› Planer
› Spring clamps (2)
› Pencil or marker
› Bandsaw
› Epoxy
› Drill press
› Drill bit sized to match pins
› Drill bit, ¼"
› Belt sander
› Sandpaper
› Wood finish of choice

If you're like me, you may have had a tendency to rip open your mail like a savage. Fortunately for us both, we now have a chance to put those days solidly in the rearview mirror. If you wish to become a bit more civilized—or know someone who might, and is in need of a gift—then here's your chance. This straightforward design would make a fine upgrade to anyone's office décor.

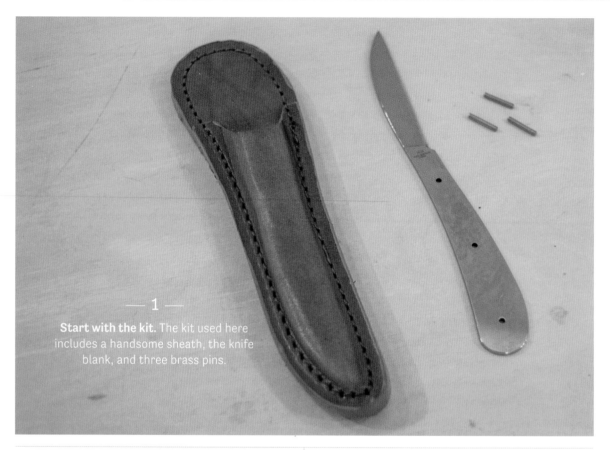

— 1 —

Start with the kit. The kit used here includes a handsome sheath, the knife blank, and three brass pins.

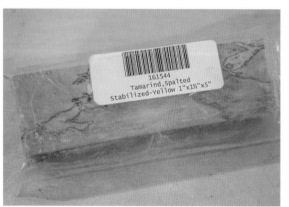

— 2 —

Choose your handle stock. Sometimes it's good to go with an eye-catching handle. The knife seen here is made from stabilized spalted tamarind. For more on stabilized wood, see page 79. To learn about spalted wood, see the box on page 143.

— 3 —

Mark out the sides of the handle. Use a straightedge to help divide the tamarind block into sections. You can cut it into two pieces, or, as shown here, divide it into four pieces so you can get 2 sets out of a single block and you'll have enough material to make two knives. Then cut to the lines at the bandsaw.

— 4 —

Draw out the handle. Lay out the knife blank to best showcase the spalted figure of the wood.

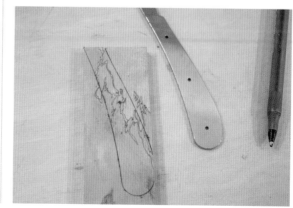

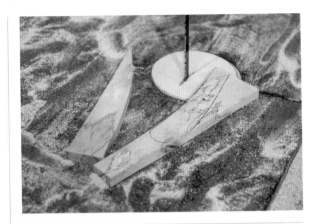

— 5 —

Cut out the profile. The bandsaw makes quick work of cutting the profile of the handle out of the thin stock.

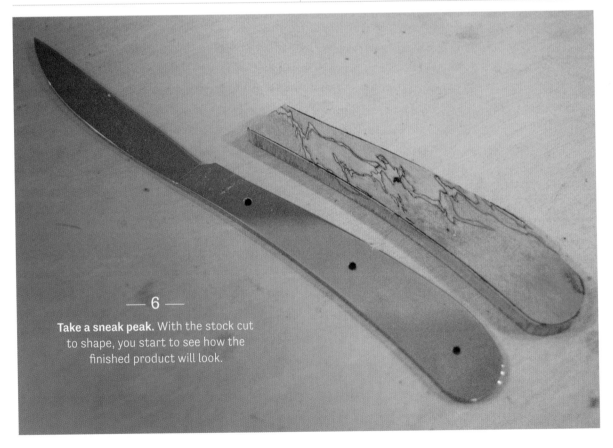

— 6 —

Take a sneak peak. With the stock cut to shape, you start to see how the finished product will look.

— 7 —
Prepare the second side. Trace the first side onto the other piece of wood to get the second side laid out. Then cut it to shape at the bandsaw.

— 8 —
Attach the first side. Mix and lay on a thin layer of 5-minute epoxy. Then secure the handle to the blade with a spring clamp. Before the glue begins to set, make sure the wood overhangs the metal at least a little on all sides.

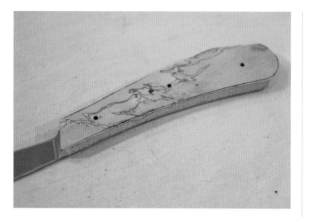

— 9 —

Get ready for the pins. Once the epoxy dries, drill holes with your drill press and a drill bit sized to match the pins. Drill the holes by going through the metal first as a guide and continuing on through the handle stock. Once complete, you should have three clean and perfectly aligned holes, as shown here.

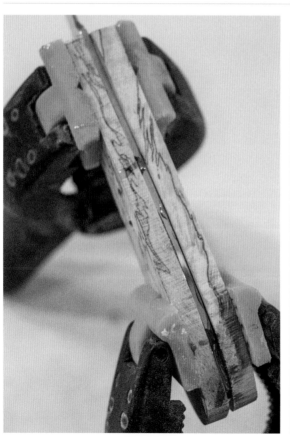

10

Glue on the second side. Apply a thin layer of epoxy and set the second side into place. A few spring clamps secure everything until the glue cures.

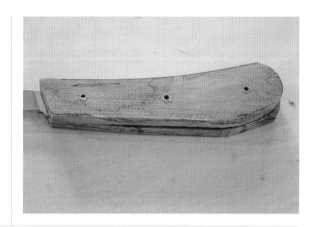

—11—

Drill out the second side. After the epoxy dries, use your drill press to drill through the holes created on side one all the way through the second side.

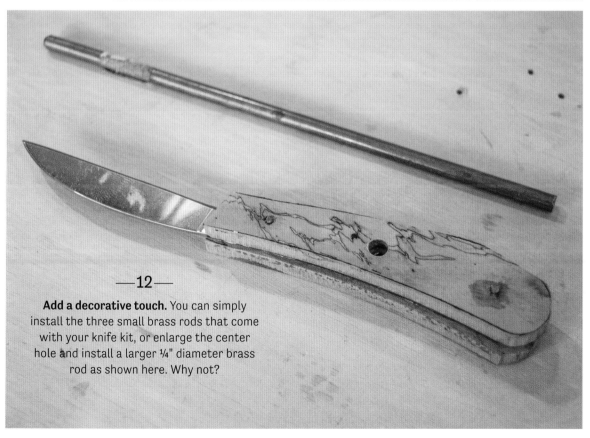

—12—

Add a decorative touch. You can simply install the three small brass rods that come with your knife kit, or enlarge the center hole and install a larger ¼" diameter brass rod as shown here. Why not?

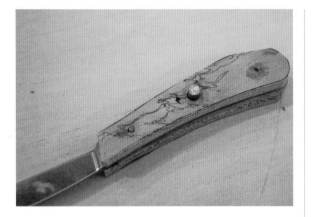

—13—

Drive the pins home. Brass is soft and easy to trim, but it's still a good idea to cut the rod only a little longer than needed so that you won't have too much excess to sand away. Then add a few drops of epoxy in the holes, set the pins into place, and tap them home with a hammer.

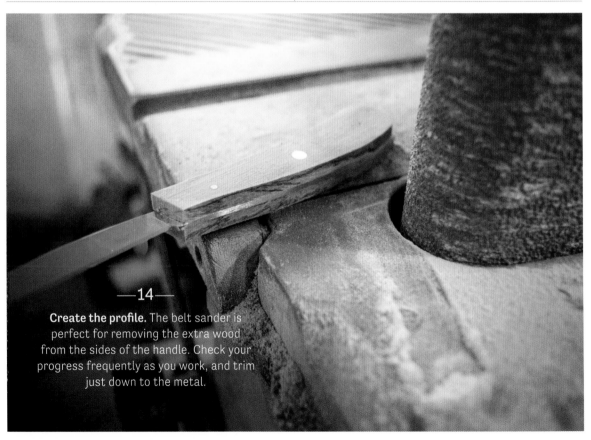

—14—

Create the profile. The belt sander is perfect for removing the extra wood from the sides of the handle. Check your progress frequently as you work, and trim just down to the metal.

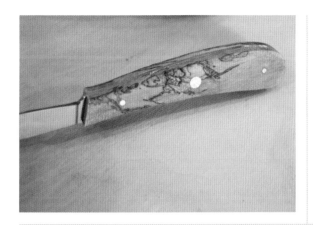

—15—

Finish it off. The belt sander is also great for bringing the brass pins flush to the wood and cleaning up the front and back faces of the handle. The edges of the handle can be softened by simply knocking off the hard edges with a piece of sandpaper. Then apply your finish of choice.

WHAT IS SPALTED WOOD?

Spalting is a form of wood coloration caused by fungi. It is generally limited to hardwoods, as most softwoods are more susceptible to rot, which degrades the wood too quickly to be of use. It is primarily found in dead trees. Typically, it presents as areas of dark lines, lacy patterns, or other very unusual features that don't quite reflect the wood's normal grain. Such wood is generally highly prized by woodworkers. Pale hardwoods are most likely to spalt; this includes birches, maples, and beeches. Small blanks of spalted and stabilized wood can be found in a myriad of dyed colors and are often used by turners. But the small blanks also are perfectly sized for creating small knife handles. Note the dust from spalted wood can cause a reaction to some, so always use a dust mask when cutting it.

BOTTLE OPENER

A custom way to pop your tops

MATERIALS & TOOLS

- Bottle opener kit
- Scales or wood of choice, 4½" x 1½" x ⅜"
- Tablesaw
- Pen
- Bandsaw
- Belt sander or oscillating spindle sander
- 120-grit sandpaper
- Epoxy
- Spring clamps
- Drill press with bit to match pins
- Random-orbit sander
- Hammer
- Desired finish

Who doesn't like a cold one every now and then? I know I do, so the idea of a custom bottle opener was too good to pass up. I was really excited about this project for another reason: a few years ago, a huge cottonwood tree in our neighborhood came down. I was bummed, because it was a big ol' granddad of a tree—gnarly, massive, and cool. The only silver lining was that I saved a few limbs for small projects. I came across a little chunk of cottonwood I'd been hoarding, and was tickled pink to finally find a use for it. Since every good project has a story behind it, I figured that this was just about perfect. Now I'll think about that great old cottonwood tree every time I reach for this opener for years to come.

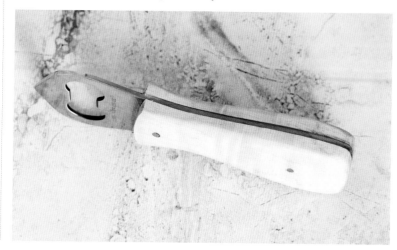

BOTTLE OPENER

— 1 —

Gather your handle material. It doesn't look like much, but this chunk of cottonwood is plenty big for this project. If you start with a block of wood, mill it to a more manageable size.

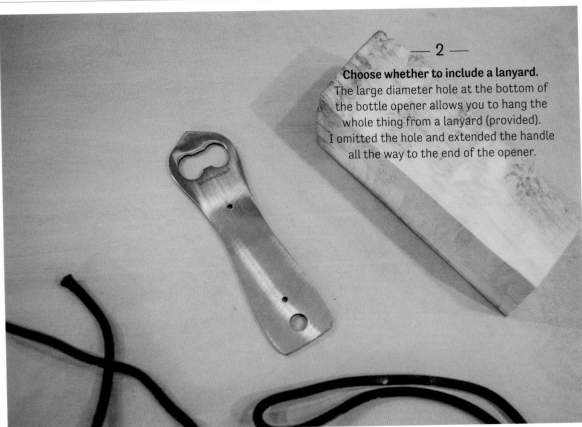

— 2 —

Choose whether to include a lanyard. The large diameter hole at the bottom of the bottle opener allows you to hang the whole thing from a lanyard (provided). I omitted the hole and extended the handle all the way to the end of the opener.

— 3 —

Trace the profile. To create the scales, trace the overall profile of the opener onto the blank.

— 4 —

Create the scales. Use a bandsaw to cut out one side of the profile. Flip the blank onto its perpendicular edge and cut two scales about ⅜"-thick. Note the placement of the lanyard hole if you choose to use it.

— 5 —

Complete the profile. Once you have two scales separated from the initial blank, finish sawing out the profile of the first scale.

— 6 —

Smooth the scale. Flatten the scale and remove any milling marks with your belt sander.

— 7 —

Complete the second scale. Once the first scale is finished, use it as a template to mark the rest of the second scale. Cut out the rest of the profile with the bandsaw and smooth it with the belt sander.

— 8 —

Begin shaping the top curve. The bandsaw is great for shaping curves, although you'll need to make sure to keep a firm grip and go "with the flow." That is, keep the workpiece properly oriented to the direction that the belt is moving so that you are always working safely. An oscillating spindle sander is another good tool for such tasks.

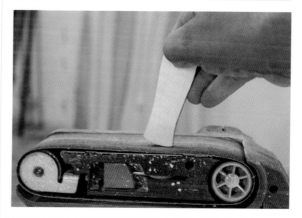

— 9 —

Trace the curve on the second scale. Use the first scale as a template for the second to easily lay out the curve at the top on the second scale.

—10—

Glue the first scale. I recommend scuff-sanding the metal first with 120 grit to help with adhesion. Spring clamps and epoxy are all you need to glue down the first scale. Wait until it is dry.

—11—

Drill the first half of the pin holes. To mark the holes in the first scale, use your drill press to drill through the holes in the bottle opener.

—12—

Attach and drill the second scale. After the second scale has been glued on, drill the holes the rest of the way through.

—13—

Sand the excess wood. A belt sander or oscillating spindle sander will make quick work of cleaning up the excess wood.

—14—

Sculpt the handle. Now, add some 3-D shaping on the handle so it isn't just a rectangular blank with eased edges. The natural place to introduce some sculpting is at the waist (the narrowest point). Hold the opener at an angle and pass it back and forth across the end of the sanding belt. Do this on all four sides of the opener.

—15—

Smooth the handle. A random orbit sander turned out to be a very handy tool for feathering out the transitions and getting a nice, smooth look.

—16—

Set the pins. Mix a bit of epoxy and set the pins with a hammer. Allow the assembly to dry about 30 minutes and then use the belt sander to quickly buzz down any excess. Finish the handle as desired.

A HANDMADE GIFT IS ALWAYS BEST

Frankly, I was already sold by the idea of a custom bottle opener. Not only do I really like the one that I made for myself, but it's a great gift idea. You could even pair it with a six pack of craft beer if the recipient is really somebody special. But in case you're still not sold, the opener can also chip ice and shuck oysters. Say what? I'm going to have to admit that I've never shucked an oyster in my life, but I just looked it up online and it doesn't look so tough. Now that I have an actual oyster shucker, I'll be shopping for bivalves this week and popping the little guys open. And you can bet that while I'm doing it, I'll be drinking a nice, cold, freshly opened beer.

CHAPTER 5

BLADE MAKING

Now that you have plenty of experience crafting knife handles to go with various blade kits, you're probably curious about creating the actual blade itself. This chapter will walk you through selecting metal for your blade, shaping it, and getting it ready to receive a homemade handle. As you can imagine, this process is a bit more involved, but don't let that intimidate you. You'll be a knife-making pro before you know it!

MAKE A KNIFE FROM SCRATCH

Create a custom blade and handle to match

MATERIALS & TOOLS

> Steel blank of choice (see sidebar on page 158)
> Pattern of choice
> Permanent marker
> Screw clamp
> Bandsaw, jigsaw, or angle grinder
> Belt sander with 24-grit sandpaper
> Glass of water
> ³⁄₁₆"-diameter brass rods
> Calipers
> Drill press with ³⁄₁₆" drill bit
> Random-orbit sander with 50-grit paper
> Scales or wood of choice, ⁵⁄₁₆"-thick and sized to fit your knife handle
> Epoxy
> Spring clamps
> Hammer
> Rasp, chisel, rotary tool, or detail sander
> Desired finish

There's nothing like making your own knife, from scratch—no kit needed! After you get the hang of this, the whole world of knife making is open to you. Truly custom knives for any use you can imagine will be within reach. Good knife steel is also easy to find— check out the sidebar on page 158 for more information.

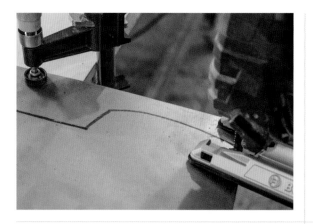

— 1 —

Rough out the blade. Find a knife you like the shape of and use it as a template. You can also find patterns online. Mark the steel with a permanent marker. Use a bandsaw or a jigsaw to rough out the knife from the rectangular blank. Use the best blade you can find, and don't plan on getting a lot of mileage from it. You can also use an angle grinder with a thin cut-off wheel.

— 2 —

Review your work. Removing waste takes a lot longer with metal than with wood, so make sure to leave as little extra material as possible. You'll be glad you did later on.

SOURCING STEEL

All steel is, as you'd probably imagine, not created equal. I recommend only working with special steel blends that are engineered for knife-making—this ensures the optimal combination of sharpness and the ability to hold an edge for a long time. If you'd like stainless steel, go with a 440-series steel. 440c is a classic, and it's hard to beat. If you don't mind a steel that will take on a patina over time, 1095 is an old favorite. You can find plenty of places to read up on steels online, and when you're ready to buy, there are a few knife-making supply stores online that will be happy to help out.

— 3 —

Shape the outside profile. The belt sander is really a workhorse for knife-making. Use 24-grit paper.

— 4 —

Begin grinding the blade edge. When the outside profile of the knife has been evened out, it's time to begin grinding down the sides of the blade. Start on one end of the blade and pass it evenly across to the other end. It's important to keep the blank moving so you don't remove material unevenly or build up too much heat in one place.

— 5 —

Continue grinding the blade. It will take a few passes on each blade edge to form the blade. Remember to start at the tip and move toward the handle in a nice, smooth arc. To keep the edge of the blade symmetrical, alternate periodically between the two sides. This will eventually create the fine cutting edge in the middle.

— 6 —

Cool the blade. The blade will heat up now and then—just dip it in a glass of water to cool it off.

— 7 —

Pause to examine the blade edge. It takes a while, but this photo shows how the material is gradually removed from the edge of the blade.

— 8 —

Continue grinding. Repeat the grinding process until the edge really takes shape. The grinding is nearly complete on this blade.

— 9 —

Measure the pins. Brass rod works well for the pins. You can even use scrap—just double-check the diameter of the rod with a set of calipers so you can match it with the correct drill bit.

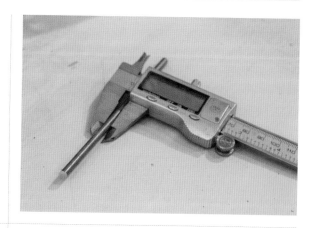

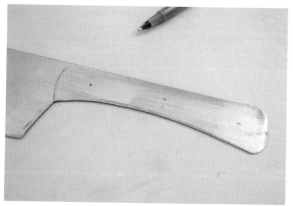

—10—

Mark the pins. The three pins are evenly spaced to create a nice finished look.

—11—

Drill the holes. Drill the holes with a drill press. If the steel is thin, as this was, you don't need to worry about lowering the speed.

—12—

Heat-treat the blade. It is critical to perform all the milling and drilling prior to heat-treating, because you won't be able to do it afterward; the steel is simply too hard at that point. This blade has come back from the heat-treater, which is evident by the slight change in color—it has kind of a smoky look.

—13—

Sand the blade. Before attaching the handle, it is necessary to sand off the patina left by the heat-treating, especially around the area where the end of the handle meets the blade. It is difficult to reach this area once the wood is adhered. A random-orbit sander with 50-grit paper works well.

HEAT-TREATING STEEL

A blade that hasn't been heat-treated is really just a knife-shaped object. I found this out the hard way by making a number of lovely knives that just didn't work very well. I then experimented with backyard forging; this method requires a lot of trial and error, plus the time and money to build a forge. Ultimately, I took my blades to a commercial-scale heat-treating facility. Such facilities often charge a minimum, but can do several blades for the price. There are also places you can mail your blades to, and they don't usually have a minimum. Carefully heat-treating blades to over 2,000°F and coordinating the temperatures is not to be taken lightly, so I highly recommend farming it out.

—14—

Select the scale material. For a simple, classic look, it is hard to beat the combination of walnut, brass, and steel, but choose any wood you like for the scales. Trace out the handle shape onto a $5/16$"-thick blank.

—15—

Cut out the scales. Used the bandsaw to cut out one handle scale and then use it as a pattern for the second.

—16—

Glue on the first scale. Epoxy and a pair of spring clamps are all you need for the glue-up. Allow to dry before proceeding.

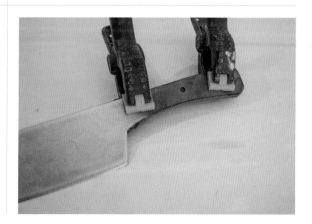

—17—

Drill the first half of the holes. Drill through the holes and the first scale. Keeping the drill press set to 90° is critical to keeping the operation precise and ensuring that the pins will fit properly.

—18—

Glue on the second scale. Mix some epoxy and glue down the second scale. You only have one chance to get it right, so make sure to align the scales neatly—trying to adjust things later will be a real pain. Try for a level of alignment that requires almost no fine-tuning after the fact.

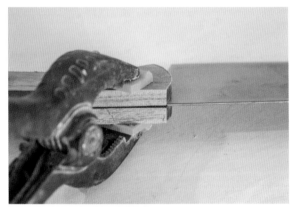

—19—

Drill the second half of the holes. Once the epoxy has cured, you can drill through the existing holes. Your drilling should look nice and clean, with no tear-out.

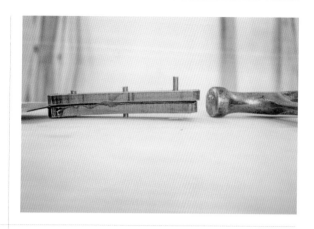

—20—

Set the pins. Filling the holes with epoxy and setting the pins into place just takes a few minutes, but feel free to breathe a sigh of relief at this stage—it feels like a bit of a milestone. Allow the epoxy to set and trim the brass rods to length at the bandsasw

—21—

Remove the extra pin material. Because brass is a relatively soft metal, you can use a belt sander to remove the extra. It goes quickly—maybe a minute or so per side.

—22—

Smooth the handle. The belt sander is the tool for the job when it comes to removing any over-hanging wood.

—23—

Sand the interior nook. The belt sander can usually reach nearly all of the inside face of the handle, too. Accessing the little nook at the top of the handle can be tricky—just use any tool in your arsenal and you'll be able to even out that last little bit. Rasps, chisels, rotary tools, and detail sanders are all good options.

—24—

Round the heel. The heel of the handle should have a nice refined feel to it. Round it over softly by rotating it over the belt sander.

—25—

Round the handle edges. As a final step, round the edges of the handle. This is a matter of personal preference—it is finished when you like the feel of it in your hand. Again, use any tools that you like to get the job done. Finish the handle as desired and sharpen the blade as you would any other.

RESOURCES

The projects in this book were made using the kits outlined below. Feel free to use your favorite brand of kit (available online and through your local woodworking shop).

8" Chef's Knife
Hock, 1/8" thick x 8" Chef's Knife Kit, #KC800

Damascus Steel Chef's Knife
Zhen, Chef's 67-Layer Damascus Knife Blank 8 1/4" L x 5/64" T, #153653

8" Slicing/Carving Knife
Hock, 3/32" thick x 8" Slicing/Carving Knife Kit, #KS800

Paring Knife
Zhen, 3 5/16" L x 5/64" T Parer 67-Layer Damascus Knife Blank, #153655

Alaskan Ulu
Wood River, Ulu Knife Kit, #77D91

Drop Point Knife
Sarge, 3 3/4" blade x 8 3/8" overall, #SK-914KIT

Drop Point Hunter's Knife
Wood River, Drop Point Hunter's Knife Kit, #EW368

Semi-Skinner Knife
Sarge, Semi-Skinner Knife Kit, #SK-907KIT

Skinner Knife
Wood River, Skinner Knife Kit 2 1/4" blade x 6" overall, #148357W

Mini Hunter Fixed Blade
Sarge, Mini Hunter Fixed Blade, 2 5/8" blade x 6 1/8" overall, #SK704KIT

Pocket Knife
Sarge, SK-405

Small Custom Folding Knife
Sarge, #SK-16KIT

Camp Hatchet
Wood River, #77D90

Desk Knife
Sarge, Desk Knife 2 3/4" blade x 6 1/8" overall, #SK-38

Bottle Opener
Sarge, #SK-40KIT

METRIC CONVERSIONS

In this book, I've used inches, showing anything less than one as a fraction. If you want to convert those to metric measurements, please use the following formulas:

Fractions to Decimals

1/8 = .125

1/4 = .25

1/2 = .5

5/8 = .625

3/4 = .75

Imperial to Metric Conversion

Length
Multiply inches by 25.4 to get millimeters

Multiply inches by 2.54 to get centimeters

Multiply yards by .9144 to get meters

For example, if you wanted to convert 1 1/8 inches to millimeters:

1.125 in. x 25.4mm = 28.575mm

And to convert 2 1/2 yards to meters:

2.5 yd. x .9144m = 2.286m

INDEX

MORE GREAT BOOKS *from* SPRING HOUSE PRESS

The New Bandsaw Box Book
ISBN: 978-1-940611-32-7
List Price: $19.95 | 120 Pages

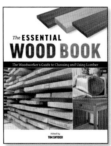

The Essential Wood Book
ISBN: 978-1-940611-37-2
List Price: $27.95 | 216 Pages

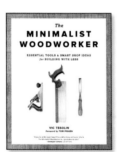

The Minimalist Woodworker
ISBN: 978-1-940611-35-8
List Price: $24.95 | 152 Pages

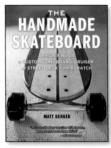

The Handmade Skateboard
ISBN: 978-1-940611-06-8
List Price: $24.95 | 160 Pages

SPRING HOUSE PRESS

Look for these Spring House Press titles at your favorite bookstore, specialty retailer, or visit *www.springhousepress.com*. For more information about Spring House Press, call 717-208-3739 or email us at *info@springhousepress.com*.